From

Christmas, 1945.

AUTHOR'S CLASS IN METALWORK AT STOUT INSTITUTE, MENOMONIE, WISCONSIN

METALCRAFT
and
JEWELRY

By

EMIL F. KRONQUIST

*Formerly Instructor in Milwaukee State Normal School and
the Washington High School, Milwaukee, Wis.*

THE MANUAL ARTS PRESS
Peoria, Illinois

Printed in the United States of America

INTRODUCTION

INTELLECTUAL education has run away with us. The balance necessary for a rounded-out culture can only be had when the practice of the arts as well as appreciation is a part of general community life. Machinery today has robbed us of the urge to be practical with our hands, but no machine has ever designed, and no design has been successful unless the material of its application was thoroughly understood by the designer.

We no longer have to produce as individuals with our hands the necessities and comforts of daily life, and this very leisure which science has given us promotes a passion for grace and satisfaction in all the things we possess. A product of manufacture must now be beautiful as well as useful. The design that goes into it must be created by one who understands the materials from which it is made. Who knows the limitations of wood, stone, metal, clay, or fabric unless he has worked in it?

The development of aesthetics was never more needed from the practical standpoint, but from the standpoint of individual happiness it is even more needed. With machinery doing the world's work there is time to spend in the daily life of all. Shall it be squandered, or will we really buy something with it? Pleasure can be bought on the outside but happiness comes from within. The flare to create beauty is rare in a mechanical age, but within all humans is a smouldering desire, the devine heritage. This is not recognized in the great system, the steam-roller process, of present-day education.

"I should like to do something worth while with my

spare time, but I know not how. The mystery of the arts baffles me." This delightful book is one of the answers, clearly opening the way, step by step, but with direct and simple approach, to the practice of metal-craft. Nothing seems to have been omitted; it is surely a complete text-book for the novice. Emil Kronquist's scholarly and thorough attack is happily void of pedantry and technical confusions. While it is food for babes, the experienced master will find many a morsel of help and potent stimulation in its illustrations and eloquent text.

The conscientious and thorough presentation of a life work such as this is might be dull but for the obvious inspiration and enthusiasm that has gone into the long hours of writing, drawing, and photography. Its thrills are many. This generous sharing of life's riches places us in this artist-teacher-craftsman's debt. He leaves his own pursuits and takes us by the hand, leading us gently but joyously into a world of beauty and a life worth while.

DUDLEY CRAFTS WATSON
Director of Extension Work
Chicago Art Institute

FOREWORD

ACCOMPLISHMENT in any art or craft is not easy, but usually we do a thing of this kind because we love to.

To really appreciate a piece of work it is essential to know how it was made. The possibilities in designing are limited to the extent of the knowledge the worker has of the medium he intends to work in.

The primary purpose of this book is to acquaint the reader with the metals chiefly used by the craftworker—silver, brass, and copper.

Simple jewelry lends itself splendidly as a medium for teaching metal-craft, and the making of useful articles for personal adornment or gifts is well within the scope of the beginner. The students' work shown in this book indicates what may be accomplished by careful and systematic guidance.

The question of design is, and always will be, the great obstacle in teaching a craft, because the creative ability of the average person is limited to an extent of discouragement. We should, however, remember that it is hardly fair to expect a student to design or plan something to be worked in a material with which he is not familiar, and little knowing its limitations. With this important fact in mind the basic outline of this book was made.

A type problem is presented and the different steps of operation are shown in a graphical sequence. The text matter explains the various tools and their uses, which are illustrated wherever necessary. Additional designs are presented for each type problem for the purpose of offering a suggestion for further study.

It is hoped some of the contents of the pages to follow will prove beneficial to the student craftworker and furnish information, and perhaps inspiration, to carry on the work as an avocation.

I desire to express my appreciation to Milwaukee Downer College and to my former students of the Milwaukee Normal Art School and Stout Institute, Menomonie, Wisconsin, much of their work being reproduced herein.

I desire also to express my appreciation to George H. Trautman, whose work is shown, and my acknowledgment of the courtesies rendered by The Gorham Co., New York; Espositer Varni Co., New York; and Ben. Hunt, Milwaukee, Wisconsin.

TABLE OF CONTENTS

PAGE

INTRODUCTION................................. 5

FOREWORD.................................... 7

CHAPTER I. ESSENTIAL PRELIMINARY INFORMATION   11

1. General rules. 2. Design. 3. Transferring a Design.
4. Scratch Awl and Burnisher. 5. Preparation of Metal.
6. Precautions. 7. Cleaning by Chemicals. 8. Baser Metals.
9. Precious Metals. 10. Carat. 11. Metal Gages. 12.
Processes.

CHAPTER II. PIERCED WORK.................... 20

13. The Watch Fob. 14. Drilling. 15. Sawing. 16. Files
and Filing. 17. Wire and Wire Drawing. 18. Hard Soldering. 19. Silver Solder. 20. Iron Binding Wire. 21. Final
Pickling.

CHAPTER III. PINS AND BROOCHES WITH SETTINGS.   33

22. The Possibilities in Designing. 23. The Close Setting.
24. The Brooch. 25. The Heat Application. 26. The Bezel.
27. Setting the Stone.

CHAPTER IV. PINS AND BROOCHES WITH LIGHT
CARVING.................................... 47

28. The Designs. 29. The Tools. 30. Chasing. 31. The
Scarf Pin.

CHAPTER V. RING MAKING.................... 61

32. Pierced Work. 33. Rings with Applied Work. 34. Rings,
Carved and Chased.

CHAPTER VI. CHASING AND REPOUSSÉ WORK   69

35. Chasing, 36. The Pitch. 37. Preparation. 38. Chaser's
Pitch Bowl. 39. Chaser's Pitch Block. 40. Heating the
Pitch. 41. Attaching the Metal to the Pitch. 42. A Chaser's

or Repoussé Worker's Hammer. 43. Making Chasing Tools. 44. Hardening and Tempering. 45. To Harden a Steel Tool. 46. To Temper. 47. Holding the Chasing Tool. 48. Preliminary Exercises in Repoussé Work. 49. The Pendant. 50. Repoussé Work on Hollow Articles.

CHAPTER VII. WIRE-DRAWING AND WIRE WORK..   97

51. The P r o c e s s of Wire-Drawing. 52. Draw-Plates. 53. Chain Making. 54. Unit Jewelry. 55. Twisting Wires. 56. Filigree.

CHAPTER VIII. STONES AND METALS—SOLDERING. 110

57. Stones. 58. Precious Stones. 59. Semi-precious Stones. 60. Hardness. 61. Birth Stones. 62. How to Order Silver or Gold. 63. Melting Silver and Scraps. 64. Rolling. 65. Composition Metal. 66. Soft Solder. 67. Flux for Soft Solder. 68. Soldering Iron or Bit. 69. Tinning Copper Point. 70. Cleaning the Bit by Dipping.

CHAPTER IX. HAMMERED WORK................ 124

71. Art Metalwork. 72. F l a t Work. 73. Planishing. 74. Rivets. 75. Process of Riveting. 76. Letter Opener. 77. Drawer Pulls. 78. The Dapping Die. 79. Lanterns. 80. Desk Set.

CHAPTER X. RAISED WORK.................... 151

81. Shallow Bowls or Trays. 82. Planishing. 83. Raising. 84. Crimping. 85. Trays and Platters. 86. Seaming.

CHAPTER XI. METAL COLORING—OXIDIZING...... 173

87. Metal Coloring. 88. Polishing. 89. Oxidizing Silver. 90. Oxidizing Copper. 91. Oxidizing Copper or Brass. 92. Bright Dip. 93. Metal Lacquer.

DEALERS..................................... 180

INDEX....................................... 183

CHAPTER I

1. **There are as a rule** several ways of executing a piece of work, whether it be gold, silver, brass, or copper, but the preliminary processes of preparing the design and the metal are about the same in each case.

The problems in this book will take the worker from the simple to the more complex, showing in many cases how the same design can be worked out by different methods.

2. **Design.** The term "design" means in its broad sense to plan something. It may be under any of the three general heads: naturalistic, conventional, or geometric.

Considerable time is usually spent on the design, and it is of the utmost importance because upon this one thing depends whether we are going to be interested in doing the work and finally admire the finished object.

A clean, accurate outline drawing should be made from the design on a good grade of tissue or tracing paper, using a pencil not too hard, but pointed sharp as a needle and kept in that condition by the frequent use of an old file or sandpaper.

3. **Transferring a Design** on to a metallic surface may be accomplished in several different ways.

Yellow beeswax is an excellent medium for transferring small, intricate designs of jewelry on to gold, silver, copper, or brass. The wax is applied to the clean surface of the metal, which has been previously heated, by rubbing

11

on a very small quantity and wiping with a clean rag to insure an even, thin film. When the metal is cold, place the tracing with the pencil lines toward the waxed surface and rub carefully with a burnisher or any hard, smooth instrument. If the metal surface was clean, with not too much wax, an exact, clear-cut duplicate of the design will be assured.

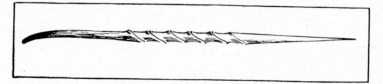

FIG. 1. THE STEEL SCRATCHER AND BURNISHER

Carbon paper can be used for most general work of larger size. The impression left on the metal surface will be greatly improved if, previous to tracing off the design, the surface is wiped with turpentine or gamboge.

4. **Scratch Awl and Burnisher.** It is necessary in most cases to scratch in the design after it has been transferred to the metal. A piece of ⅛-inch square tool steel 6 inches long, filed to a taper, one end slightly curved and polished, will prove an effective and useful tool. (Fig. 1)

5. **Preparation of Metal.** Annealing is to render a piece of metal soft by the application of heat. This may be done by the gas blow torch with foot bellow (Fig. 2), the Bunsen burner, a large-size alcohol lamp (Fig. 4) or gas (Fig. 5) used in connection with a mouth blowpipe. (Fig. 6) The ordinary gas plate may also be used to good advantage for heating smaller pieces of metal.

6. **Precautions.** Silver and copper may be plunged into a liquid red-hot without the risk of cracking.

Gold of less than 14 carats should be allowed to cool before throwing it into a liquid.

Brass or any alloy is a treacherous metal; it should be heated slowly and allowed to cool gradually as there is

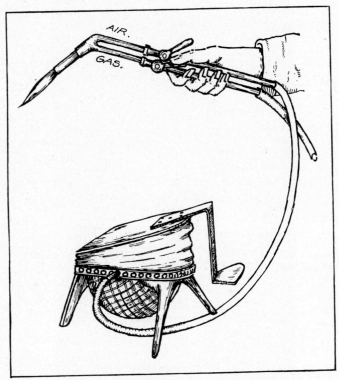

FIG. 2. THE BLOW-TORCH AND FOOT-BELLOWS

always danger of cracking the metal when it is subjected to a sudden blow or extreme change of temperature.

7. **Cleaning by Chemicals.** "Pickle" is the name used for the cleaning solution, which consists of sulphuric acid

Fig. 3. Gold Pendant Carved and Chased
by Author

and water; about one part of acid to fifty parts of water makes a satisfactory solution for generalwork. In preparing the pickle add the acid to the water.

Fig. 4. Alcohol Soldering Lamp

A pickle pan or jar, a vessel made of copper or lead (Fig. 7) is very serviceable, as frequently the acid must be heated in order to quicken its action upon the metal.

Allow the annealed metal to remain in the pickle until clean, which takes only a minute or two if the acid solution is boiling. Silver will turn pure white with a matte surface that is excellent to draw on, or transfer designs to.

Copper or brass is scoured with water and pumice powder, or a kitchen cleanser such as Dutch Cleanser or the like. Use a brush in a circular action which will insure a uniformly finished surface. After scouring, rinse in water; then dry the metal with a rag or heat it slightly over a blue flame.

Fig. 5. Gas Burner for Soldering

8. **Baser Metals** such as copper and brass are splendid mediums for the craftsman and adapt themselves admirably for decorative metalwork.

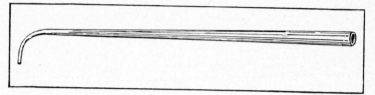

Fig. 6. The Mouth Blowpipe

Copper in many ways is the most useful of metals. Among its valuable properties may be mentioned its extreme ductility, which enables it to be drawn into fine wire, while its toughness enables it to be rolled or beaten

Fig. 7. A Pickle Pan

into thin sheets. From an artistic point of view, copper is a beautiful metal. Many different colors can be produced when it is subjected to various chemicals or heat treatments. It is a perfect medium for the enameler to work in. It is sold in sheets 30 by 60 inches. any thickness, soft, half-hard, and hard. It melts at 1,996 degrees Fahrenheit.

Brass is an alloy consisting mainly of copper and zinc. In its older use the term applied rather to alloys of copper and tin, now known as bronze. It is a rich yellow shade and an excellent material for the craftsman. It possesses a high tensile strength and ductility, but care must be exercised in the execution of the work; frequent and careful annealing while work is in progress is necessary. It can not be forged red-hot and must not be quenched, as cracking may occur at the most unexpected moments. It is sold in sheets 12 by 60 inches, any thickness, soft, half-hard, and hard—the latter is also known as "spring brass." Brass (containing 25 per cent of zinc) melts at 1,750 degrees Fahrenheit.

9. **Precious Metals,** silver and gold, were known from the earliest times and are of great importance as "noble" metals for articles of value—coinage, ornamentation, jewelry and silverware.

Silver is one of the most beautiful of all metals—no metal is better to work in. Pure silver is snow-white and capable of taking a high polish, but it is very soft and not practical in making durable objects. However, it is quite often used for bezels or settings for delicate stones. It is fused at 1,873 degrees Fahrenheit.

Sterling silver is a name given to an alloy of silver and copper, 925 parts of fine silver and 75 parts of copper, also called 925–1000 fine. This alloy is used in America and England in the production of jewelry and silverware. It is sold by refiners and assayers (see list of Dealers) in any quantity, shape, or gage. Bars of silver can be purchased at leading banks.

Gold, valued from the earliest ages on account of the

permanency of its color and luster, when pure is nearly as soft as lead. It is the most malleable of all metals; it is also extremely ductile—one grain may be drawn into a wire 500 feet long and it has been hammered into leaves less than a millionth of an inch in thickness. Fine gold is too soft for all ordinary purposes and is usually alloyed

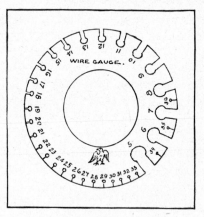

Fig. 8.   The Wire Gage

with other metals such as silver and copper to render it serviceable for the manufacturer and craftsman. Gold alloyed with copper has a reddish color; if alloyed with silver, it is yellow or green. The fusing point is at 1,947 degrees Fahrenheit.

10. **Carat.** The word "carat" means a twenty-fourth part when used in connection with gold. It expresses the proportion of gold in an alloy. Thus, gold 18 carats fine is 18/24 or ¾ pure gold. The carat is also a unit of weight for gems and is equal to 3.166 grains.

Gold as well as silver is bought from banks or refiners and assayers.

11. **Metal Gages.** Many different metal gages are on the market for measuring the thickness of sheet-metal and wires. No standard exists, but the Browne & Sharpe wire gage is known by all dealers in America. It is important to specify the name and number of the gage in purchasing baser or precious metals.

Baser metals, such as copper or brass, are sold in sheets, while precious metals may be purchased by the ounce or cut to specific size. The thickness is measured by the slot the metal or wire fits into. The hole at the bottom of the slot is just for clearance. (Fig. 8)

12. **Processes.** Most metalworkers agree that the best result is obtained when a student is led on by carefully selected problems, for it is not only necessary to learn the process, but a certain amount of practice must also be acquired in order to understand and master the uses of the various tools. Only through diligent practice can the higher exercises of the craft be achieved.

Each problem with the various processes and tools used will be taken up, separately in the pages that follow.

CHAPTER II

PIERCED WORK

13. The Watch Fob. (Fig. 9) Make a clean outline drawing on tracing paper or tissue paper, transferring by the beeswax method (see Sec. 3) onto a piece of sterling silver, 18 gage, Browne & Sharpe. Scratch in the design carefully with a steel point, as the work will require a good deal of handling, and the soft pencil line may otherwise be lost.

14. Drilling. If any inside metal is to be removed, holes must be drilled. The hand drill (Fig. 11) is well suited for this work. A small-size twist drill may be used, but it is still better to make the drill as follows: Heat a needle to make the steel soft, then break off the point and flatten one end. Now harden it again by making it red-hot and quenching in water; rub it on a piece of emery cloth to make it bright. Temper it to a light blue color by drawing it carefully through a soft flame. Sharpen on an oilstone to the shape shown in Fig. 12 and apply a little water or oil to the drill point while each hole is being drilled. This type of drill point is known to the trade as a Swiss drill and may be purchased from jewelry supply stores.

15. Sawing is done with what is known as a jeweler's saw; a saw-frame five inch deep with a no. 0 blade is well suited for all-round work. (Fig. 13)

Saw blades are purchased by the gross or dozen lots. They are highly tempered steel blades essentially made for metal cutting but can be used for cutting wood also.

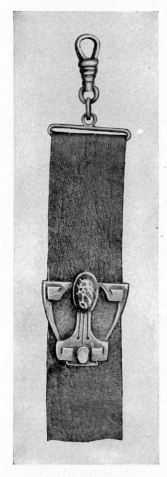

Fig. 9. Watch Fob

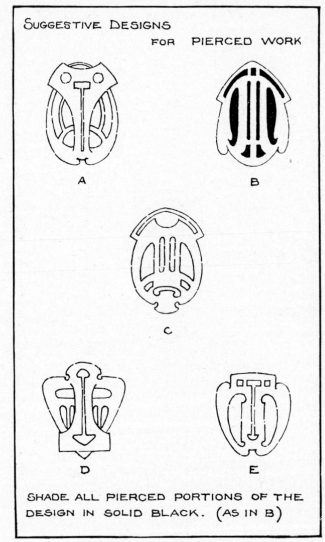

FIG. 10. DESIGNS FOR WATCH FOBS

The finest saw-blades made, No. 000000, are about the thickness of a horse-hair. The heaviest blades No. 6, make

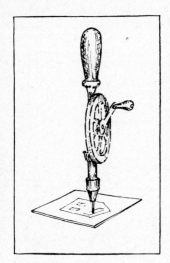

a saw cut about $\frac{1}{64}$ of an inch wide and are only suitable for cutting thick-gage metal. The blade should always be placed in the saw-frame with the teeth pointing toward the handle and clamped at the top of the frame first, then the frame is sprung and the blade tightened in the clamp near the handle. (Fig. 14)

Fig. 11. The Hand Drill

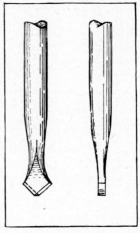

Fig. 12. Drill Points

There should be a fairly high tension on the blade as it cuts more accurately and does not break quite as readily as a sloppy or loose blade.

In using the saw, hold it in an almost perpendicular position; since the teeth all point down, the saw only cuts on the down stroke. A little practice soon will enable one to do creditable work. A V-shaped piece of wood screwed to the bench (Fig. 13) should be part of the worker's equipment.

16. **Files and Filing.** Files are known by their shape, cut, and size. The teeth are like a series of small chisels

cut at an angle to the sides of the file. (Fig. 15) It cuts only on the forward stroke. The length of the file is the distance from the heel to the point; the tang, or part that goes into the file handle, is not included in the length.

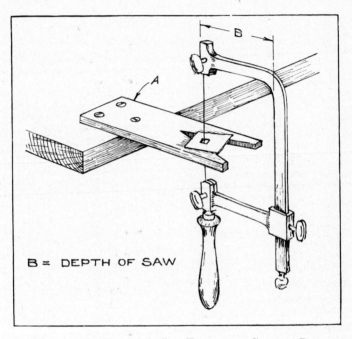

FIG. 13. THE JEWELER'S SAW-FRAME AND CUTTING BOARD

Fig. 16 shows the end views of sections of files. In filing, the tool often gets clogged with chips of metal and should be cleaned frequently with a wire brush called a file-card. After the sawing out it is necessary to true up the irregular edges left by the saw. A needle file $3\frac{1}{2}$ inches long, of the shape best suited to the outline should be used for this purpose.

Many different methods are used in fastening ornaments to ribbon or leather.

17. **Wire and Wire Drawing.** Unlimited combinations and shapes and sizes of wire can be produced, and the

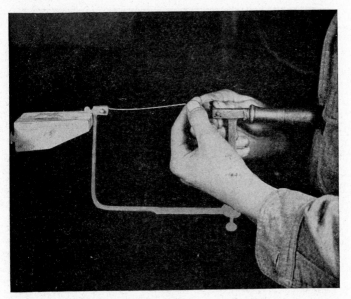

Fig. 14. The Saw Blade Being Clamped into Place

decorative adaptation by the craftsman presents a rich field for study. Gold and silver wire can be purchased in any gage. (See chapter on "Dealers")

The tools needed for the process of reducing the size of wire are a draw-plate and a heavy pair of pliers. (Fig. 17) A wire may be reduced to any size or shape by pulling it gradually through a series of holes, one after the other, annealing frequently. The danger of burning the wire during annealing may be lessened if the wire is coiled up in a bundle (Fig. 18) and placed on a charcoal or asbestos block and the mouth-blow brought into use.

Steel draw-plates can be had with holes of different shapes—round, square, half-round, or triangular.

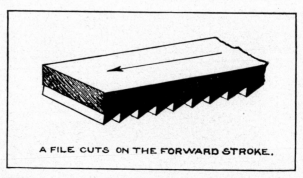

A FILE CUTS ON THE FORWARD STROKE.

Fig. 15. Enlarged View Showing Action of File Teeth

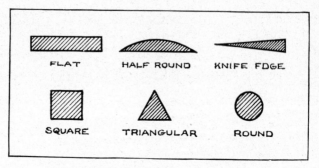

FLAT   HALF ROUND   KNIFE EDGE

SQUARE   TRIANGULAR   ROUND

Fig. 16. Cross-Sections of Files

The top and the back crossbar of the fob are made by drawing a piece of silver wire to a 15 gage. Roll a few links on a wire brad or fine nail as shown in Fig. 19; then separate by cutting the links thus formed with a jeweler's saw. The long upper bar to hold the ribbon is bent with a

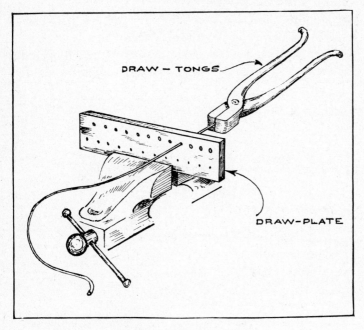

FIG. 17. DRAWING WIRE

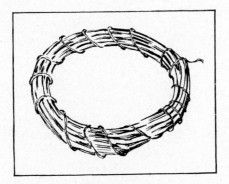

FIG. 18. A COIL OF WIRE TIED UP FOR
ANNEALING

pair of round-nose pliers. (Fig. 20) Prepare and assemble on a charcoal block as shown in Fig. 21. Care must be taken that all the joints that now are going to be hard-soldered are clean and in contact with each other.

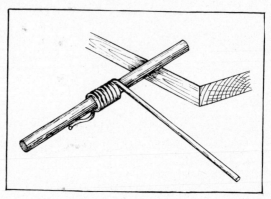

Fig. 19.   Making Round Links

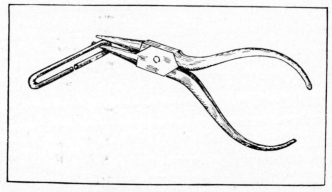

Fig. 20.   The Round-Nose Pliers in Use

18. Hard-Soldering. The art of soldering may be divided into two classes, hard-soldering and soft-soldering. The latter process will be explained later. Hard-soldering means the uniting of separate parts by the use of an alloy solder which melts or fuses at a lower temperature than the work to be soldered. It is always necessary to bring the work to a red-hot heat in hard-soldering.

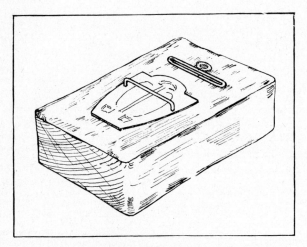

FIG. 21. WORK PREPARED FOR SOLDERING ON THE CHARCOAL BLOCK

When metals are heated, a scale called oxide forms on their surface. To prevent the oxide from forming in the process of heating, a substance called a "flux" is applied to the joint or surfaces. The flux forms a coating, which prevents oxidation and also acts by dissolving the oxide. There are many fluxes, each of which has a particular use.

The flux used for hard-soldering is borax. Take a piece of lump borax, rub this in a few drops of water on a slate (Fig. 22) until a thin, white, milky fluid is produced. Cover the joint to be soldered with this flux after the edges have been closely fitted. Cut the silver solder as

shown in Fig. 23; then place the tiny pieces on the edge of
the borax slate and cover them with the flux.   By means
of a camel-hair brush, the small pieces of solder are

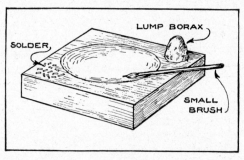

FIG. 22. HOLLOW SLATE FOR GRINDING THE
BORAX

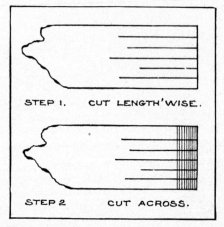

FIG. 23. METHOD OF CUTTING SOLDER

placed on the joint to be soldered.   The work is then
gently warmed in the flame of a blowpipe to evaporate the
water in the borax. When this is dry apply a stronger flame

over the whole work to get it thoroughly heated. Now a brisk flame may be directed upon the chips of solder which will run as soon as the work has been brought up to the melting temperature of the solder. It is very important to get a quick heat, as an oxide will otherwise form on the metallic surface in spite of the borax. The solder will always run toward the hottest place. As a general rule, not always, boil out the work in the sulphuric pickle, after each soldering, and rinse in water, as perfect cleanliness is absolutely necessary to success.

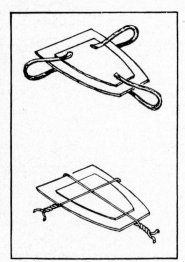

FIG. 24. CLAMPING OR TYING UP A PIECE OF WORK

19. **Silver Solder** is pre-pared or purchased (see list of Dealers) in different grades, hard- and easy-flowing. One melts at a higher temperature than the other, which is often desirable when many details are to be soldered on the same piece of work. A loam or paste made from jeweler's rouge and water, or moulding sand or whit-

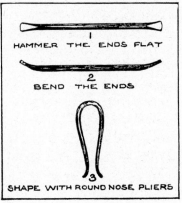

HAMMER THE ENDS FLAT

BEND THE ENDS

SHAPE WITH ROUND NOSE PLIERS

FIG. 25. HOW TO MAKE SMALL IRON CLAMPS

ing is useful as a protective in fine soldering where seams or previously made joints must be protected.

20. **Iron Binding Wire,** also called annealed iron wire, is used extensively to tie up separate units to be soldered. Three different gages, Nos. 15, 22 and 28, should be on

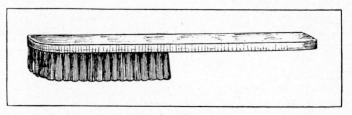

Fig. 26. Wire Scratch Brush, Brass or Steel

hand. Fig. 24 shows two methods of tying up a small job before soldering. The clamps are made from the 15 gage wire as shown in Fig. 25. Before boiling off in pickle remove all iron wire or clamps to prevent discoloration. When the tool work is finished emery cloth or paper is used on the surface and edges. Flat work can be placed face down on No. 00 emery paper on a level bench top.

21. **Final Pickling.** Scrub the work with fine sand or a scratch brush and water (Fig. 26); then anneal and boil in the pickle solution. If it does not turn pure white repeat the process of scrubbing, annealing, and pickling. For finishing see Chapter XI.

CHAPTER III

Pins and Brooches with Settings

22. The possibilities in designing hand-wrought jewelry are increased many-fold when we can deal with three dimensions. The setting of precious or semi-precious stones gives the article a commercial as well as an artistic value.

In applying one piece of metal on the top of another by means of solder or rivets, more relief is given to the work. This added material gives more thickness, which in turn enables one to carve and shape or mold the design.

The brooches in Figs. 27, 28, and 29 are problems involving the making of a simple setting and soldering one piece of metal on the top of another. Work of this

FIG. 27.   SILVER BROOCH
By Miss G. Schmidt

nature is not beyond the ability of the average student; care, however, must be exercised in not making the design too intricate.

Let us assume that the stone to be used is cut in what is known as a cabochon shape; that is, a stone having a smooth curved surface. (Fig. 30) Translucent and opaque stones are usually cut in a cabochon shape which brings

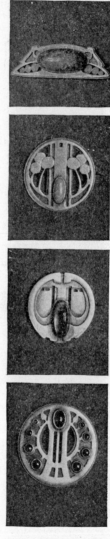

FIG. 28. SILVER
PINS

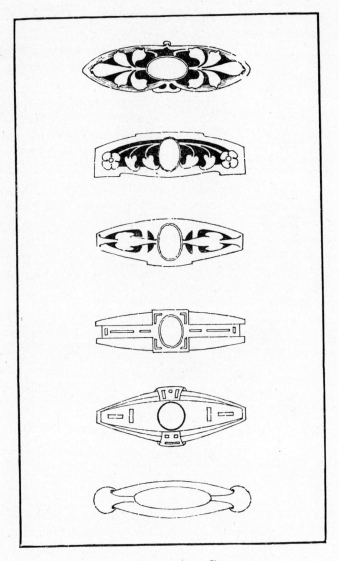

Fig. 29. Designs for Brooches

out their color and luster. For places to purchase stones see the list of Dealers.

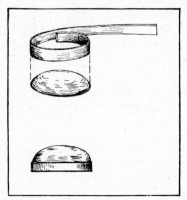

FIG. 30. MAKING A CLOSE OR BOX SETTING

23. The Close Setting, also called box or bezel setting is the simplest form of setting to make. Cut a band of silver about one eighth of an inch wide, gage 28, Browne & Sharpe. Bend the strip so that it fits closely around the stone. (Fig. 30) Mark the exact place of the seam and cut to size. The flat-nosed pliers are now used to squeeze it gently into shape. (Fig. 31) The ends

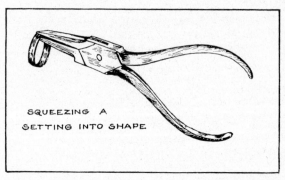

SQUEEZING A SETTING INTO SHAPE

FIG. 31. SQUEEZING A SETTING INTO SHAPE

must meet perfectly before any soldering is attempted. There must be contact between the two ends to unite them. Placing the bezel on the charcoal block as shown in Fig. 32, with an iron staple (made from binding wire) to prevent it from rolling off, cover the joint with borax and a tiny piece of solder and apply heat with the mouth blow-pipe. (Fig. 33) Care must be taken not to get it too hot, as it is thin material and easily melted. When it is properly soldered place the bezel on a tapering steel mandrel or small-horn anvil and tap it with a light hammer(Figs. 34 and 35) until it is true and round.

A setting can always be made larger by tapping it with the hammer on the mandrel, but if it is made too large it will have to be cut open and a piece taken out, then re-soldered.

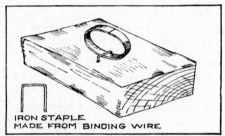

IRON STAPLE
MADE FROM BINDING WIRE

Fig. 32. Soldering a Bezel on a Charcoal Block

The setting can be squeezed to any shape with the round- or flat-nosed plier after the trueing up. Level the bezel thus made by rubbing it on an 8- or 10-inch flat mill file. (Fig. 36) The stone must fit perfectly and not too tight; pressure exerted on the stone while trying it in the bezel may result in chipping it.

24. **The Brooch** (Fig. 37) is cut or pierced from two pieces of silver, the lower part from gage 20 and the upper from gage 22. Trace the top part of the design, transfer to the silver and saw it out, (Fig. 37-A) File all edges clean and true and scrape the under side clean. This is now soldered to the piece of 20 gage silver. (Fig. 37-B) When two pieces of this character are to form the ornament, thought should be given to the part which forms the lower layer of the design. The surface should be

finished with No. 00 emery cloth. Apply borax on both
pieces of metal before clamping together. The solder
must be put sparingly on the outside edges where any
surplus can easily be removed afterwards.

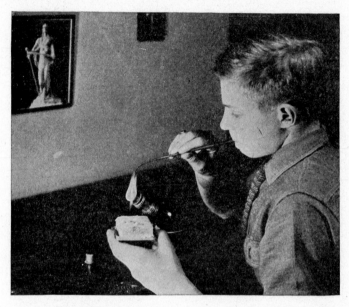

FIG. 33. SOLDERING WITH ALCOHOL LAMP

25. **The Heat Application** should be quick to make the
solder run through. Remove the iron clamps or wire, then
boil in the pickle solution and rinse in water. The lower
part of the design is now pierced with the saw (Fig. 37-C),
and all edges and the top surface are filed clean and smooth
and finished with No. 00 emery cloth.

26. **The Bezel** which has been previously made is now
dipped in the borax solution and placed in position on the
brooch. (Fig. 37-D) Two or three small pieces of solder

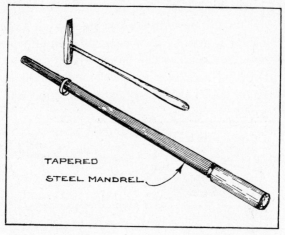

Fig. 34. Stretching a Bezel on a Steel Mandrel

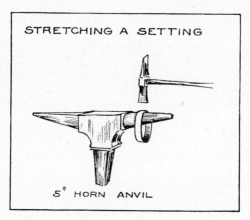

Fig. 35. Jeweler's Horn Anvil in Use

are placed on the inside of the bezel, touching both the bezel and the base. If the borax is allowed to dry before heat is applied, there is not much danger of the bezel

being moved out of place. The center part shown in black
in Fig. 37-E is now sawed out, leaving enough metal near
the setting for the stone to rest on. Catch and joint are
very rarely made, as they can be purchased in any kind of
metal at a low price in any jeweler's supply house. A
small piece of solder is placed next to the joint and catch

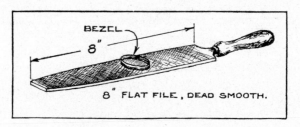

FIG. 36. LEVELING UP THE BEZEL

after they have been properly cleaned and borax applied.
It is advisable to raise the object from the charcoal block
so that the flame can be directed under the work. If the
heat is directed on the joint or catch, the solder will flow
upon them. The whole object must be heated up gradually, and the flame then concentrated where solder should
run. Solder will always flow towards the hottest spot.

The brooch is then pickled, rinsed, and scratch-brushed.
The pin is fitted into the joint and a piece of wire is filed
to a taper (Fig. 38) and forced through joint and pin; the
projecting ends of wire are sawed off or clipped off close
to the joint with a pair of cutting pliers.

27. **Setting the Stone.** A place to hold the work firmly
while the stone is being set is made from a piece of wood
about 1½ inches square and 4 inches long with some dry
orange shellac or chasing pitch melted on one end of
block. (Fig. 39) While this substance is still soft press the

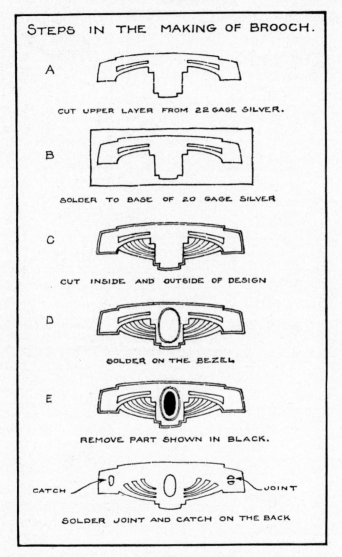

STEPS IN THE MAKING OF BROOCH.

A

CUT UPPER LAYER FROM 22 GAGE SILVER.

B

SOLDER TO BASE OF 20 GAGE SILVER

C

CUT INSIDE AND OUTSIDE OF DESIGN

D

SOLDER ON THE BEZEL

E

REMOVE PART SHOWN IN BLACK.

CATCH — JOINT

SOLDER JOINT AND CATCH ON THE BACK

Fig. 37. Design of a Brooch and Several Steps in
Its Making

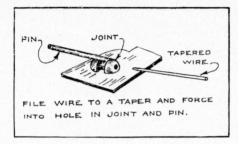

PIN
JOINT
TAPERED WIRE

FILE WIRE TO A TAPER AND FORCE INTO HOLE IN JOINT AND PIN.

FIG. 38. FORCING TAPERED WIRE INTO JOINT AND PIN

SHELLAC OR PITCH

FIG. 39. BLOCK WITH CEMENT

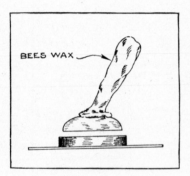

BEES WAX

FIG. 40. FITTING STONE INTO BEZEL

FIG. 42. SETTING A STONE

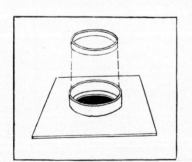

FIG. 41. A LOOSE INNER BEZEL

work into it, then allow it to get cool and hard. This provides a good base where the work is held firmly. The stone is fitted into the bezel by pressing a small piece of beeswax on the stone (Fig. 40); this grips the stone so that it may be tried in the bezel and easily removed. The rim of metal is now filed down to the proper height, which is determined by the height of the stone. Care must be

FIG. 43. PUSHING TOOLS USED
FOR SETTING A STONE

taken not to get the bezel too low as there must be enough metal to cover the edge of stone. If the stone sits too low it may be raised or heightened by inserting an inner bezel. (Fig. 41) The edge of the bezel is pushed or hammered toward the stone, working at opposite points as 1, 2, 3, 4 in Fig. 42. The irregularities left from setting can be smoothed out with a burnisher.

By heating the work slightly over an alcohol lamp, it can easily be removed from the shellac or pitch. If anything adheres to the under side, it can be dissolved with alcohol or turpentine. If the work is greased a trifle before it is placed on the pitch, it can be removed clean.

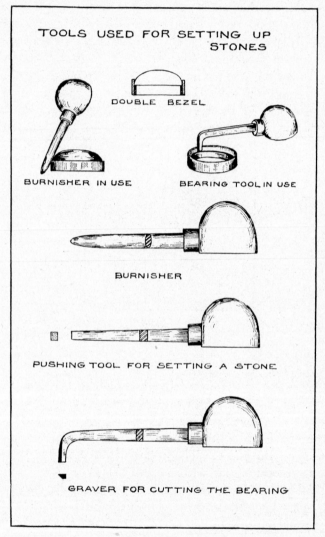

FIG. 44. SETTING A STONE, AND TOOLS USED

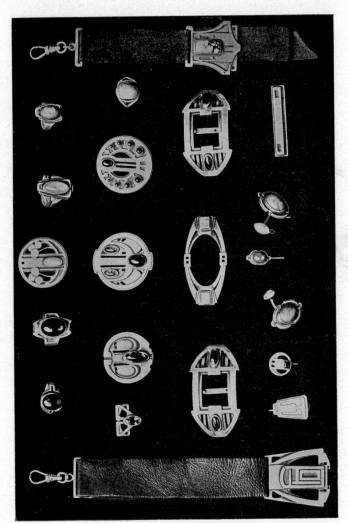

FIG. 45. WORK BY THE STUDENTS OF THE MILWAUKEE STATE NORMAL SCHOOL

Fig. 46. Silver Work by Students—Bar Pin, Watch
Fob, Shoe Buckles

CHAPTER IV

Pins and Brooches with Light Carving

28. **The designs** shown in Fig. 47 all require a little carving to make them interesting. The process will be described by using a type problem. (Fig. 48) The upper part of the design is tranferred by the beeswax method described in Sec. 3 to a piece of silver of 20 gage, and carefully pierced out with a jeweler's saw No. 0. It will now have the appearance of the top illustration in Fig. 48. All inside edges must be filed clean before they are soldered on to the lower base, which ought to be a slightly lighter gage metal, about 22. It should be clamped on or tied up with light iron binding wire as shown in Fig. 24 care being taken that the two surfaces to be soldered were cleaned and free from dirt and grease. The silver solder should all be placed on the outside, as it will run through if sufficiently heated and leave smooth inside edges. The same kind of bezel or setting is made as in the first problem and soldered in place in a similar manner, the solder placed on the inside of the bezel and allowed to run out. The work should now be boiled in the pickle solution, which cleans it and dissolves all borax. The outside metal is sawed off, also the inside of the setting, leaving enough for the stone to rest on.

The work must now be fastened to the pitch block (Fig. 39) for the purpose of holding it while it is being carved. Heat the pitch over an alcohol lamp and shape it with a wet thumb and forefinger to fit the work. Now grease the back of the work with a small amount of oil and heat it

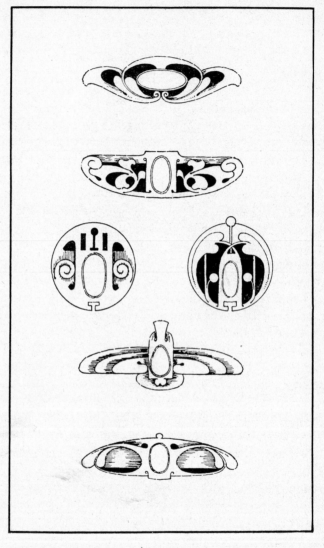

FIG. 47. BROOCHES. DESIGNED FOR LIGHT CARVING
AND CHASING

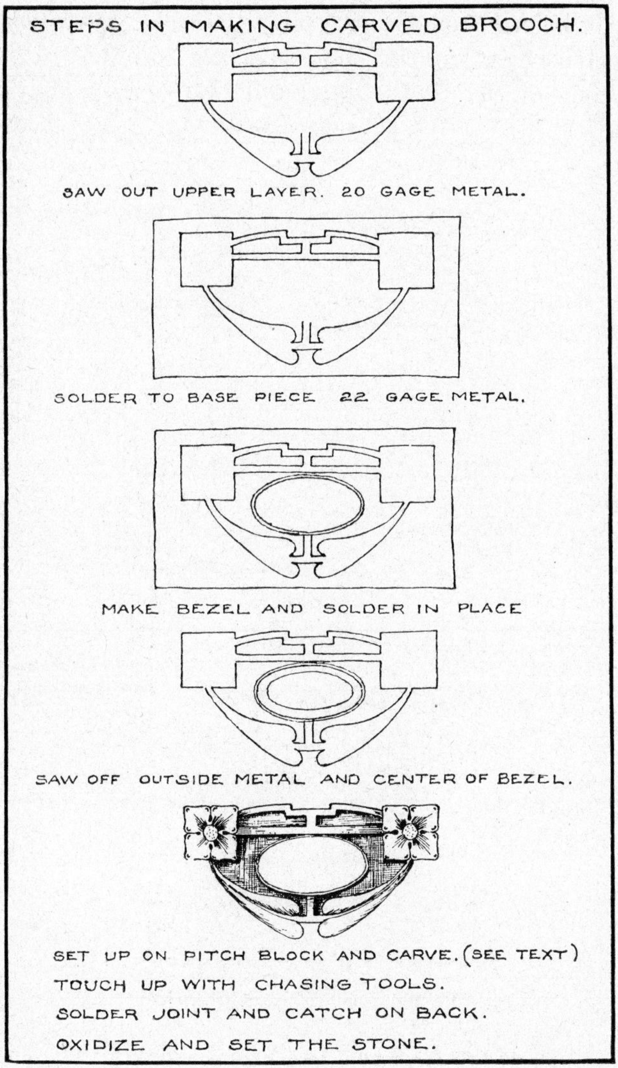

STEPS IN MAKING CARVED BROOCH.

SAW OUT UPPER LAYER. 20 GAGE METAL.

SOLDER TO BASE PIECE 22 GAGE METAL.

MAKE BEZEL AND SOLDER IN PLACE

SAW OFF OUTSIDE METAL AND CENTER OF BEZEL.

SET UP ON PITCH BLOCK AND CARVE. (SEE TEXT)
TOUCH UP WITH CHASING TOOLS.
SOLDER JOINT AND CATCH ON BACK.
OXIDIZE AND SET THE STONE.

FIG. 48. PRINCIPAL STEPS OF OPERATION IN MAKING A BROOCH

slightly before attaching it. This will cause it to stick to the pitch better, and at the same time it will also cause it to come off cleaner and more quickly when it is finished.

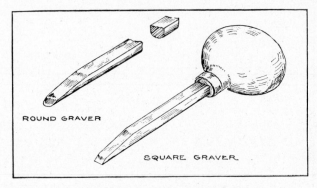

FIG. 49. THE GRAVERS USED FOR METAL CARVING

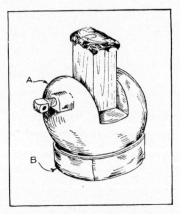

FIG. 50. THE ENGRAVER'S BALL

29. **The tools** required for metal carving are called "gravers" and can be purchased in numerous shapes and sizes. However, a ⅛-inch flat and a ⅛-inch round graver

are all that are needed for this work. (Fig. 49) The tool should be sharpened on a fine oilstone in very much the same manner as a chisel is sharpened. Remember that good work can never be done with dull tools.

The object of carving is to shape or mold the design by cutting away part of the metal. Here one's own concep-

Fig. 51. Work Being Carved. Attached to Pitch Block and Held in the Engraver's Ball

tion or interpretation of the design enters in. The pitch block is held firmly in an engraver's ball (Fig. 50) by means of a set-screw. This ball is placed in a ring (Fig. 50-B), made from an old piece of belting, where it can be turned in all directions. The graver is held in the palm of the right hand and the point of the thumb should rest on the work and serve as guide for the tool. The left hand clinches the block firmly as shown in Fig. 51. The metal is removed chip by chip until the desired shape is obtained.

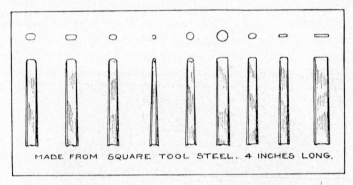

MADE FROM SQUARE TOOL STEEL. 4 INCHES LONG.

Fig. 52. A Few Useful Chasing Tools

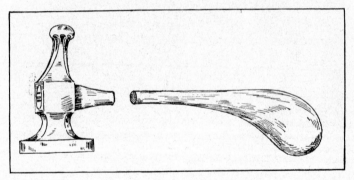

Fig. 53. Chasing Hammer

The cutting marks left by the gravers are removed by file, scraper, or chasing tools.

30. **Chasing** is a name applied to a process whereby the metal surface is treated, decorated, or shaped with the use of punches called "chasing tools" (Fig. 52) and a

small chasing hammer, (Fig. 53). A few chasing tools will
suffice for simple work of this character. Cut ⅛-inch
square tool steel into 4-inch lengths and file to a taper.
Shape one end to forms shown in Fig. 52. The surface of
the work is tooled over to give it a hammered texture.
The method of holding the tool and hammer is shown in
Fig. 55, and the process explained fully in Chapter VI.

FIG. 54. GOLD BROOCH CARVED AND CHASED
BY AUTHOR

The small balls or beads for the center of the flower are
made by fusing two small pieces of silver on a charcoal
block. A perfect circular bead is obtained by melting the
metal in a smooth, round depression in the charcoal block,
a little borax solution being applied beforehand. If many
beads of the same size are required, cut links from a coiled
piece of wire and fuse. This will result in a uniform size of
beads. To solder the ball in the center of the flower, a
small piece of solder is first fused in the cavity made;
then the ball is placed in the depression and the whole

brooch heated until solder runs on the ball. The joint and catch are soldered in place next. The work is now boiled in the sulphuric-acid solution and scratch-brushed, then oxidized. The stone is set as explained in Sec. 27.

FIG. 55.   AN ARTIST AT WORK CHASING A SILVER BOWL
By courtesy of the Gorham Co., New York

31. The Scarf Pin. The main attraction in a scarf pin is usually the stone. Great care should be exercised in building up the design around the stone. The problem of making any of the pins shown in Fig. 56 is not difficult but one must have had considerable practice in manipulating

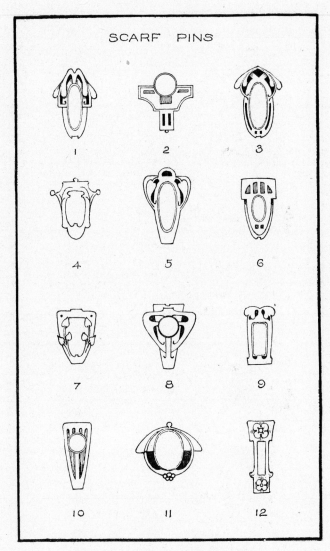

FIG. 56. DESIGNS FOR SCARF PINS

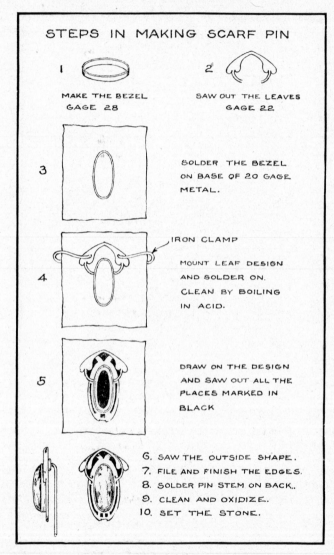

STEPS IN MAKING SCARF PIN

1　MAKE THE BEZEL GAGE 28

2　SAW OUT THE LEAVES GAGE 22

3　SOLDER THE BEZEL ON BASE OF 20 GAGE METAL.

4　IRON CLAMP

MOUNT LEAF DESIGN AND SOLDER ON. CLEAN BY BOILING IN ACID.

5　DRAW ON THE DESIGN AND SAW OUT ALL THE PLACES MARKED IN BLACK

6. SAW THE OUTSIDE SHAPE.
7. FILE AND FINISH THE EDGES.
8. SOLDER PIN STEM ON BACK..
9. CLEAN AND OXIDIZE.
10. SET THE STONE.

Fig. 57. A Scarf Pin in the Making

the jeweler's saw. Small work always requires more patience and greater care in execution than larger work.

Assuming scarf pin No. 3 in Fig. 56 is to be made, proceed by making the single bezel for the stone from 28 gage metal as previously explained. Saw out with a No. 00 jeweler's saw the top layer, which in this case consists of

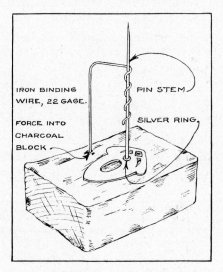

Fig. 58. Method of Holding Pin Stem in Place While Soldering

the two leaves with stems. A 22 gage metal will be suitable for this. The bezel and leaves are fitted carefully together. The bezel is next soldered on the base of a 20 gage metal which has been thoroughly cleaned with emery cloth. The leaves are placed next and tied in position with fine iron binding wire or clamps and soldered. The pin is now boiled in the diluted sulphuric acid solution and the balance of the design drawn on and sawed out. The black places are cut out first, then the inside of the bezel, leaving enough for the stone to rest on. Finally the outside is cut to shape, and the saw marks filed off on edges and finished with No. 00 emery cloth. The steps of the operation are shown graphically in Fig. 57. The scarf pin stem is usually made from German silver wire, gage 18 and 3 inches long, because this metal is somewhat harder than sterling silver and does not bend quite as readily.

File the wire flat on one end and make a ring of silver wire to fit the stem. When this ring is soldered on to the base it adds great strength. (Fig. 58) The pin stem is soldered on in an upright position, held in place by a piece of iron wire, 22 gage, which has been forced a little way into the charcoal block. This arrangement will prevent the wire from absorbing more than the minimum amount of heat while being soldered on. Clean by boiling in acid solution and scratch-brushing. The pin stem is bent to proper shape by holding it next to the base with a pair of round-nose pliers and bending it into position with the fingers. The oxidation or coloring of the work may be done either before or after the stone is set; it depends largely upon what kind of stone is being used. Some stones are porous and soft, such as corals or pearls; others contain large proportions of minerals that are sensitive to the oxidizing solutions, such as malachites or azurites, which are carbonate of copper, a form of high-grade copper ore. Work holding such stones should be oxidized before the stone is set, or great care must be taken in not getting any of the oxidizing agent on the stone.

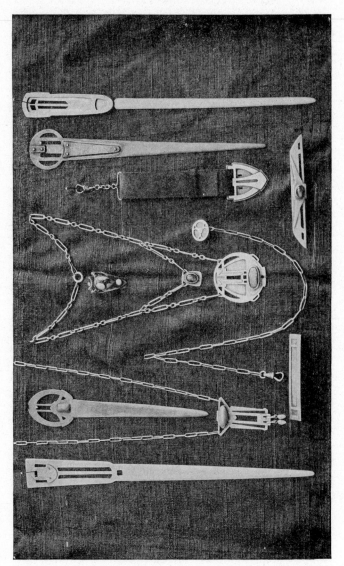

Fig. 59. Work by Students of the State Normal School, Milwaukee, Wis.

Fig. 60. Silver Cross

CHAPTER V

RING MAKING

32. **Pierced Work** should first be practiced by the student. Not until that has been mastered should more elaborate designs be attempted. The size of the ring must be known first. This is found by using a ring gage. The length of the circumference of the ring can be measured by using a narrow strip of paper. A stone is usually the central feature of a ring. For a start it is well to choose an oblong and not too wide a stone; then what is known as a box setting can be used to hold the stone. Make a carefully drawn tracing of the design and transfer it to a piece of 18 gage silver. Now scratch in the design with a steel point and saw the outside contour. The ring blank is then filed accurate and clean. Then bend the ring by placing it across a shallow groove in a block of wood and tapping with a round piece of iron or a ring mandrel and a mallet to give it the first curvature. (Fig. 61) Now hammer the ends together and saw through the joint with a jeweler's saw. This will insure a perfect joint, which is then ready to be soldered. It is not necessary to try to make the ring perfectly round before it is soldered.

The soldering is performed as explained before on the charcoal block with mouth blowpipe or torch. Quick, even heat is essential. If solder runs to one side of the ring it is because one side has become hotter than the other, for solder will always run to the hottest place, or it may be the joint has sprung apart. If that is the case set it cool and force the ends together for there must be

61

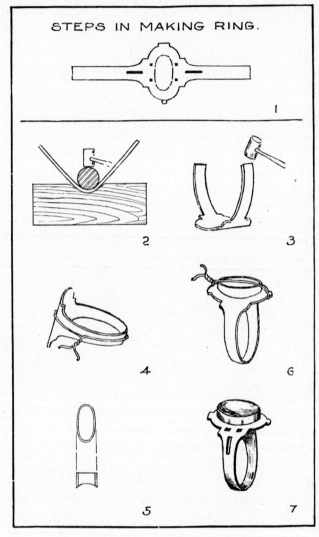

STEPS IN MAKING RING.

1

2

3

4

6

5

7

Fig. 61. Bending a Ring Blank and the Successive Operations

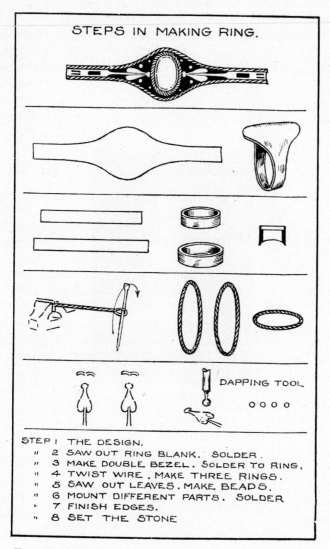

STEPS IN MAKING RING.

DAPPING TOOL

STEP 1 THE DESIGN.
  "   2 SAW OUT RING BLANK. SOLDER.
  "   3 MAKE DOUBLE BEZEL. SOLDER TO RING,
  "   4 TWIST WIRE . MAKE THREE RINGS.
  "   5 SAW OUT LEAVES . MAKE BEADS.
  "   6 MOUNT DIFFERENT PARTS. SOLDER
  "   7 FINISH EDGES.
  "   8 SET THE STONE

FIG. 62. RING DESIGN WITH SIMPLE APPLICATION WORK

contact between the two pieces to solder them. Clean it in the pickle and place it on the ring mandrel and hammer it until it takes a round shape. Reverse it once or twice on the mandrel to prevent it from taking a cone shape as the ring mandrel is tapered. It is advisable to procure a hardened ring mandrel with standard graduation of sizes, similar to the one shown in Fig. 34.

Fig. 63. Scarab Ring, Carved and Chased

The bezel for the stone must now be made. File the lower side to fit the curvature of the ring, place it where it belongs and tie it to the ring with a piece of iron binding wire (Fig. 61, step 6). Place the silver solder inside of the bezel and solder on. Drill holes for the different places to be pierced, also one inside the bezel; saw out an oval but have enough metal for the stone to rest upon. All edges are filed clean and finished with emery paper. The setting is filed down to proper height to fit the stone. Anneal the ring and boil in diluted sulphuric acid, then set the stone as previously described. For oxidation see Chapter XI.

33. **Rings with Applied Work.** There are numerous possibilities in simple ring making by using twisted wire or leaves and flowers. To make a ring as in Fig. 62 cut

FIG. 64

with the saw the outside shape from 20 gage silver. File the edges, bend and solder together. Make a double bezel to fit the stone; file it to conform to the shape of the ring and solder in place. Double up a piece of 24 gage wire and twist it. Anneal and cut three pieces, making one ring to fit around the bezel and two separate rings the size of the largest diameter of ring, bent to fit the outline; then solder on. Cut the leaves from somewhat thinner silver; dap up from the back on a block of wood or lead to give them a slight relief; then file the outline clean and accentuate the midribs. They are now fitted in place and soldered on to the ring. Fuse small pieces of silver on the charcoal block to form the beads, as previously explained.

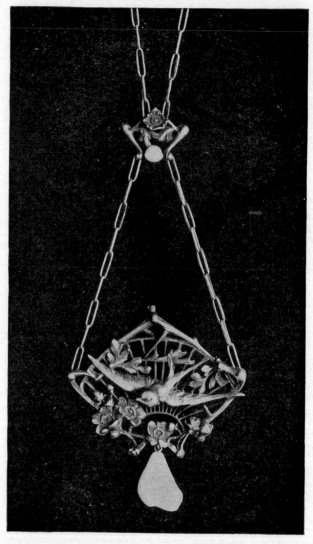

FIG. 65. PENDANT. SWALLOW AND WILD ROSE DESIGN.
CARVED AND CHASED BY AUTHOR

It is well to finish all the soldering on one side of the ring before turning it to solder the other half. Boil out in pickle solution; file the bezel down to proper height and set the stone. This may be done by holding it in a ring clamp (Fig. 92) while the metal is pushed over the stone, or it may be slipped on the tapered ring mandrel.

34. **Rings, Carved and Chased.** The rings (Figs. 63 and 64) are made from heavy-gage metal, about No. 12, soldered together, and stretched on the ring mandrel to size. The double bezel is made and the place marked on the ring blank where it eventually will go. The design is now worked or modeled into shape with the aid of carving tools (graves). The final touches are put on with the chasing tools, the ring being embedded in pitch while this work is going on and held clamped in on the engravers' ball (Fig. 50).

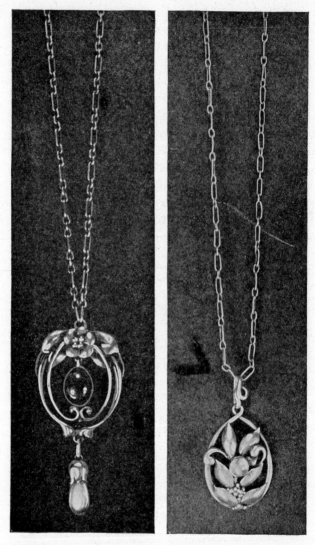

Fig. 66. Silver Pendants with Moon Stones

CHAPTER VI

Chasing and Repoussé Work

35. Chasing is the art of enriching a metal surface by means of using steel tools or punches called "chasing tools" and a hammer called a "chasing hammer." The surface treatment or touching up of a casting to remove the rough-

Fig. 67. Using the Bunsen Burner
for Heating the Pitch

ness is included in this name also. Repoussé, meaning in French "driven back," is the art of raising or modeling a design upon a sheet of metal into high or low relief with the aid of hammer and punches without removing any of the metal. The term "embossing" is often erroneously used. This latter process consists of embossing by mechanical means such as stamping, and therefore is not considered an art. Repoussé is of ancient origin; wonderful and noteworthy examples are to be seen in many of our museums. It was, however, not until the middle of the sixteenth century that Benvenuto Cellini (1500–1571), the famous goldworker and chaser of Italy, brought the art to the highest point of excellence by the production of many masterpieces, some of which are still to be seen in the European art collections.

The elementary principle of the method, after the due preparation and annealing of the metal, is to affix the metal plate to a "pitch block" by warming the pitch with a soft gas flame, such as a Bunsen burner (Fig. 67) or an alcohol lamp, until it becomes plastic or dough-like. The metal is then oiled slightly on the side that is going against the pitch, and is heated and attached. When the metal and pitch have become cool, the design is drawn or transferred upon the metal. (Fig. 68, Step 1)

The outline of the design is now indented into the metal by means of a hammer and steel punch called a "tracer" —a blunt tool resembling a chisel. Sharp tools would be liable to cut the metal and cause injury for the process to follow. (Step 2)

The metal is now taken off the pitch, annealed, and cleaned. The outline of the design is now visible on the reverse side of the metal and will serve to guide the worker in hammering it up into proper relief. (Step 3)

The metal is again attached to the pitch, this time with face down, and the design is now hammered up into proper relief with blunt chasing tools. The object is to raise enough metal so that there will be plenty to model the design from. The metal is again removed from the pitch, annealed, and cleaned. (Step 4)

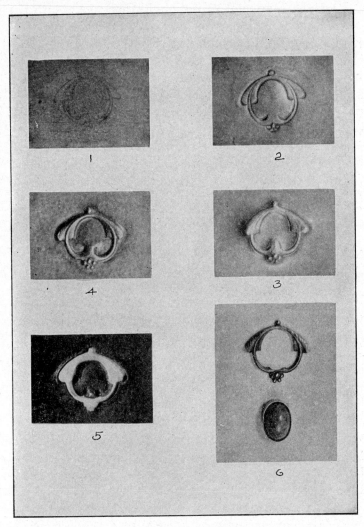

FIG. 68. SHOWING THE DIFFERENT STEPS IN MAKING A SCARF PIN IN REPOUSSÉ WORK

Reattach the metal to the pitch, then model into the desired shape. To put feeling and expression into this requires careful study and much practice. (Step 5)

If it is a piece of jewelry, as in this case, the design may be sawed out with a jeweler's saw, the setting for the stone soldered into place and the edges finished with needle files and emery cloth. The pin is then soldered on to the back as previously described. Set the stone, then oxidize.

36. The Pitch. There is no substance that can take the place of pitch as a base for the metal while the design is being executed in repoussé or chased work. It is composed of:

Pitch...1 lb.
Plaster of paris or whiting............................2 lbs.
Tallow.. 1 oz.

This mixture can be made harder by adding powdered resin, or softened by adding more tallow; common candles will do. The kind of pitch that is best suited for this work is what is known as crude Swedish pitch; however, pitch that is purchased at shoemakers' supply houses answers the purpose. (See list of Dealers)

37. Preparation. Melt the pitch in a pot (not tinned) over a slow fire. Add little by little the plaster of paris or whiting, stirring it continually. It is important that there be no moisture in the latter, as it will otherwise boil over. When this has been thoroughly mixed the tallow is melted and added. This compound, while being sufficiently hard, is elastic, solid, adhesive, and easy to apply and remove. Pitch which has been used before works much more freely than new or newly prepared pitch.

38. Chaser's Pitch Bowl. A chaser's pitch bowl (Fig. 69) is a hollow cast-iron half-ball filled with pitch. It is about 6 inches in diameter and rests in a ring made from 1½-inch old belting, or on a sandbag. The spherical shape

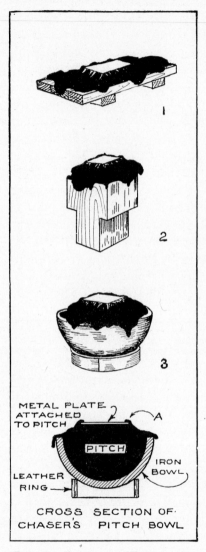

FIG. 69. DIFFERENT WAYS OF AT-
TACHING METAL PLATE TO PITCH

combined with its weight renders this very useful, as it can be turned into any convenient position the chaser may desire, and it is firm and solid to strike on.

39. **Chaser's Pitch Block.** This can be made in many sizes; the important thing is to make it heavy enough and to have plenty of pitch piled on top. If placed on a sand-bag it responds well to the blow of the hammer with only little vibration. Fig. 69 shows another type of wood block with pitch attached to top. This block, however, must be screwed into an engraver's ball (Fig. 50) to hold it firm. This style of pitch block is very handy and practical for small work as it can be released quickly and held over an alcohol lamp when it becomes necessary to heat up the pitch or turn over the work.

40. **Heating the Pitch.** This process demands the greatest care, as any scorching by excessive heat will cause the pitch to lose its adhesiveness. The gas blow torch (Fig. 2), the Bunsen burner, or alcohol lamp are well suited for this process.

41. **Attaching the Metal to the Pitch.** Warm the surface of the pitch without burning it and, having previously greased the back of the metal very slightly (that is, the side which is to come in contact with the pitch), place the metal on the pitch and press down gently. If there should be any doubt as to adhesiveness, subject the whole to additional heat quickly and apply light pressure again. There is a "knack" about this operation, but a little practice will soon overcome any difficulty. It is a very important part of the chaser's work to be able to set up his work properly and to avoid getting air bubbles below the surface of the metal upon which he is to work. The pitch should be brought over the edges of the metal, as shown in Fig. 69 at A, to keep it firmly fixed.

42. A Chaser's or Repoussé Worker's Hammer (Fig. 53) can be purchased at any jewelers' supply house. This necessary tool has a broad flat face about ⅞ inch in diameter and a round-nosed knob which is very useful for

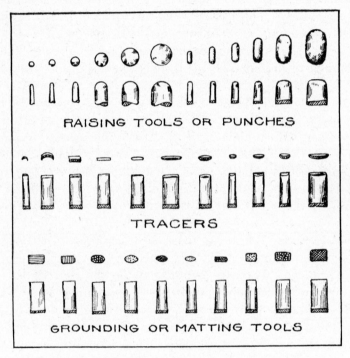

Fig. 70. Chasing Tools, the Most Important Shapes

many different purposes. The handle should be of a convenient length, about 9 inches, and made from a piece of straight-grained hard wood. The greater part of the handle must be thin and slender to give it elasticity for rapid hammering. It is a great comfort to have the butt of the handle pear-shaped; it gives a good grip and enables the worker to bring the full weight of the hammer into the blow.

43. Making Chasing Tools. The punches known as "chasing tools" (Fig. 70) are made from a selected grade of steel called "crucible steel" and often spoken of as "tool steel." This can be bought by the foot length in an iron store and is made square, round, and hexagonal in shape. The square and round steel is best adapted for the making of chasing tools. It is well to have on hand several sizes so that a particular shape can be made when needed: $\frac{3}{32}$, $\frac{1}{8}$, $\frac{5}{32}$, and $\frac{3}{16}$-inch round and square stock are good sizes to have on hand. Cut the steel with a hack-saw, or notch it with a file and break into 4-inch pieces. Avoid having the punches too long; a short tool is manipulated more easily and has a better touch than a long one, due to less vibration while being hammered upon. Before beginning to shape the tools it is well to make them red-hot and lay them aside to cool slowly to insure a softened condition before filing. There are many distinct forms of chasing tools but the great number of tools required by the chaser and repoussé worker is due to the many different kinds of work he is called upon to do; this is quite unnecessary to the beginner. The forms shown are useful tools for a start.

File the steel blank in a vise to a taper with an 8-inch bastard file. When it has taken the general form, screw it into a small hand vise (Fig. 71) and finish to desired shape with an 8-inch smooth flat file and emery cloth. To give the tool point a matte finish, hammer it on a piece of emery cloth. It is very essential that the central axis between the two bevels be kept absolutely even and true, as the tool will otherwise feel springy and make it difficult to true a line or control it. Sharp-cornered tools should be avoided; make them blunt and smooth. The object is to stretch the metal back and forth, not cutting it or reducing it in thickness, which sharp tools would naturally do.

44. Hardening and Tempering. The peculiar characteristics of steel, except the very lowest grades, are that when the metal is heated to a little more than cherry-red and suddenly quenched in water or oil it becomes exceedingly hard, and that by subsequent heating and cooling

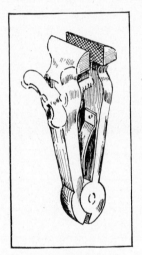

Fig. 71. The Hand Vise

the hardness may be reduced to any degree that is desired.

45. To Harden a Steel Tool. The shape must first be obtained; then cover the part to be hardened with a little soap. This precaution prevents scaling of the metal. The steel is then brought to a bright red heat and plunged instantly into water. This makes it hard and brittle.

46. To Temper. Rub the steel bright on a piece of emery cloth; then draw it through a soft flame (alcohol or gas) slowly. Notice the changes of color; when it reaches a deep straw-color plunge it into water. This operation of reheating after the hardening process is also called "drawing." The first color noticeable is a faint yellow; this indicates that the steel has lost some of its hardness and has become toughened. After the yellow it takes a blue color; after that it passes into a stage where it is soft

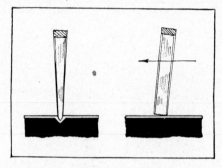

FIG. 72.   CHASING TOOL TRACING A
LINE

again. Drill points, gravers, and scrapers may be hardened and tempered in the same manner.

47. **Holding the Chasing Tool.** It is a very important thing to learn how to hold the chasing tool in the proper manner. (Fig. 55) Notice the end of the third finger rests on the metal as a pivot with the small finger pointing out. It is no easy matter to get perfect control of the tool, but by persistent practice it can be acquired and a wonderful touch developed. A line is always traced toward the worker, the blow of the hammer vibrates the tool and sets it in motion when it is properly guided.

48. **Preliminary Exercises in Repoussé Work.** Not much in the field of art can be accomplished without study

and practice. This is especially true of chasing where the mastery of directing the punches and judging the blow of the hammer means everything. For the beginner it may be well to attempt a little practice work. Attach a piece of thin annealed copper or brass (gage 26 B. & S.) to the pitch block as previously described. Design a border composed of straight and curved lines and watch the effect that is produced on the side of the metal that is embedded in the pitch. This is done with chasing tools called "tracers" or "liners." Tracers are punches made to resemble chisels at first, then the sharp edges are made blunt with fine emery cloth or a file because the object is to stretch the metal and not to cut it. (Fig. 72) Tracers are made with edges straight or more or less curved. The ornaments shown in Fig. 73 are made in a similar way, all on the reverse side of the metal. Flower studies made in this way are comparatively simple as they give the worker great freedom of action. This simple type of chasing, however, demands imagination; as the work is really done from the back side, every depression made on the metal will show up in relief on the other side. This kind of chasing is done mostly with punches having rounded surfaces called "planishers," oval or rounded modellers. The lettering in Fig. 73 is made entirely from the back side also. Lettering is of course more difficult as greater accuracy is required but it is well within the scope of the beginner to attempt.

The surface decoration on the walnut jewelry box (Fig. 74) is made of copper. The outline of the design is traced in with the chasing tools on the pitch block. The shaping or modeling is done also on pitch but from the reverse side, the pitch being somewhat warm to make it give more easily. The entire design is pierced out with the jeweler's

Fig. 73. Practice Work in Repoussé Made
Entirely from Back Side of Metal

saw. The bell button and brooch (Figs. 75 and 76) are made in a similar way.

The back comb (Fig. 77) is a piece of repoussé work, hammered up on gage 22 silver, worked alternately from the front and back. It is frequently necessary to turn such work many times on the pitch before it has taken its

FIG. 74. JEWELRY BOX, WALNUT, WITH APPLIED METAL WORK

final shape. It is then sawed out, and filed, and settings are soldered in place.

49. **The Pendant.** This type of work can be elaborated upon to a great extent. It is always composed of a central piece suspended in some way. Avoid the use of machine-made chains, for invariably the good looks of a hand-made piece of work is spoiled by hanging it on a chain of this kind. The designs shown in Fig. 78 involve only the processes which have been used in the making of the

brooches. The stones, however, are often suspended so that they hang free and reflect more of the colors of the stone. The pendant may be made so that the central part slides on the chain, or the chain may be attached to the principal piece in a permanent manner. Stones, such

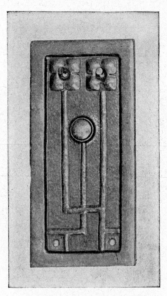

FIG. 75. BELL BUTTON PLATE

as corals, amethysts, jades, lapis lazuli, amber, azurite, or malachite all make up favorably in silver and form pleasing contrasts of value with the metal.

The pendant in iris design (Fig. 79) gives an idea of what may be done in repoussé work. It is not often made in this fashion as it is one of the more difficult types of work This, however, was hammered up from a piece of 24 gage metal in the manner described previously. The pendant (Fig. 80) is a simple piece of repoussé work beaten up from 22 gage metal with an opal swinging in the space and a pearl attached between the leaves. This type of work is explained and shown in steps. (Fig. 68)

The brooches (Fig. 81) are all executed in repoussé in 22 gage metal. After the setting for the stone has been

Fig. 76. Silver Brooch with Rose Malachite. By Author. Repoussé Work

soldered in place, the brooch must be provided with joint, pin, and catch.

Stick pins (Fig. 82) are made in repoussé. Small work is always more difficult to do as a good deal of skill must be developed before the delicate lines and forms can be modeled on the embossed piece with the chasing tools.

The two panels (Figs. 83 and 84) for a jewelry box are made in repoussé high relief. Work of this kind must be

annealed at each turning of the metal to prevent cracking.
Great care must be exercised as only blunt tools can be
used in getting the metal up to proper height.

50. **Repoussé Work on Hollow Articles.** It would be
impossible to raise a design into relief on a hollow vessel

FIG. 77. SILVER BACK COMB WITH OPAL, PEARL, AND JADES,
MADE IN REPOUSSÉ BY AUTHOR

or bowl in the manner just described; another method of
procedure is adopted. It requires the use of a simple but
wonderful tool called a "snarling iron." (Fig. 86) It can
easily be made by bending the ends of a piece of steel at
right angles and filing one end to a suitable round knob
shape. Shops as a rule have different shapes and sizes of

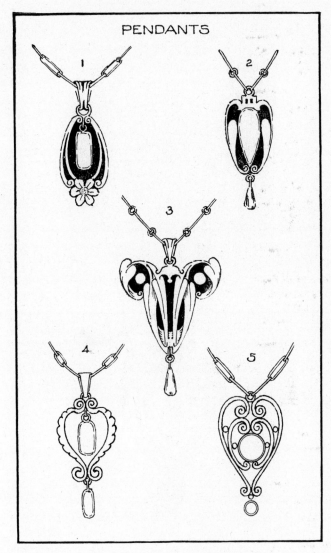

FIG. 78. PENDANT DESIGNS

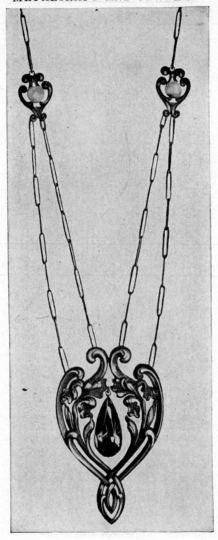

Fig. 79. Pendant, Iris Design in Repoussé Work. Designed and Made by Author

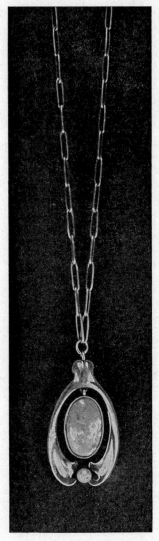

FIG. 80. SILVER PENDANT
WITH OPAL AND PEARL.
REPOUSSÉ

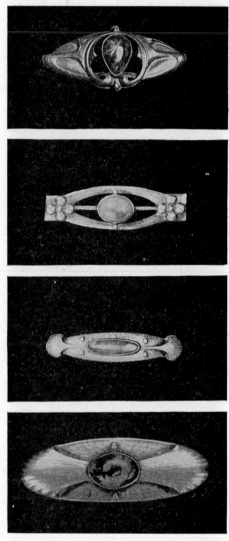

Fig. 81. Four Brooches in Repoussé
Work

these snarling irons according to the class of work to be done. The design is first drawn upon the vessel, then the snarling iron is brought into use. The operator holds the cup as shown in Fig. 87. The taps or blows delivered at one end of the iron will cause it to vibrate at the other end,

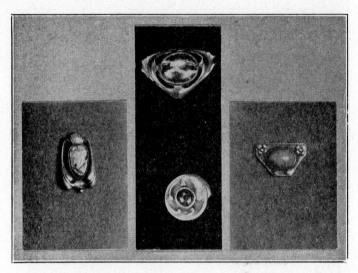

FIG. 82. SCARF PINS IN REPOUSSÉ

and by skillfully shifting the vessel, as the design demands, a rough relief will be gained.

The work is now filled with pitch and when cool the surface is treated very much the same as in flat repoussé work. The outline is traced and the background chased down; this leaves the design in bold forms, as will be noticed on the silver cup. (Fig. 88) There must be plenty of material driven up so that the ornament or figure can be modeled into form. The object is held in position on a sandbag in order to protect the surface from damage.

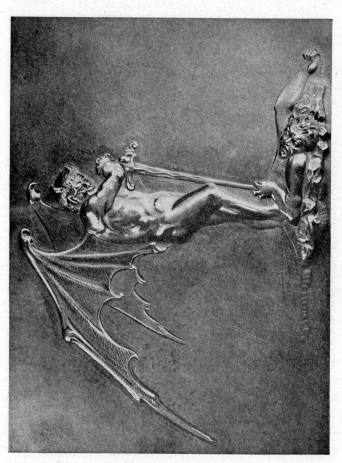

FIG. 83. TOP PANEL FOR JEWEL BOX IN REPOUSSÉ WORK, BY AUTHOR

FIG. 84. SIDE PANEL FOR JEWEL BOX IN REPOUSSÉ WORK, BY AUTHOR

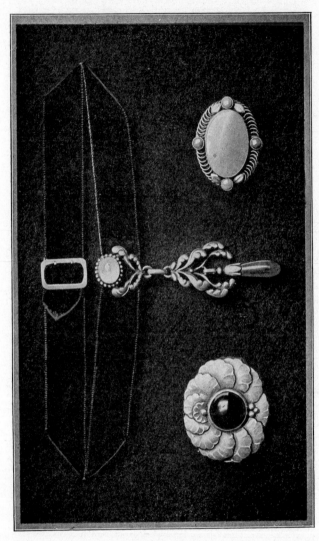

FIG. 85. SILVER PENDANT WITH MOONSTONE AND CORAL DROP. SILVER BROOCH WITH
AMBER CENTER, REPOUSSÉ. SILVER WIRE BROOCH, AMBER AND MOTHER-OF-PEARL.
By Oscar Kronquist

When the decoration is finished the pitch is melted out by application of heat, and the cup is cleaned by turpentine or gasoline, or it may also be sent through the fire and

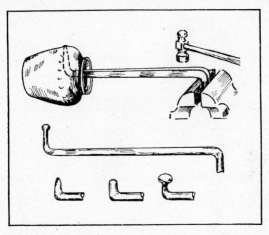

Fig. 86. The Snarling Iron in Use and Various Shapes of Same

annealed—this process will burn the remaining pitch to ashes. It is then ready for the finishing process. The child's drinking cup shown in Fig. 89 was made by the method just described.

Fig. 87. Raising Ornaments on Vase by the Use of
the Snarling Iron
By courtesy of The Gorham Co., New York

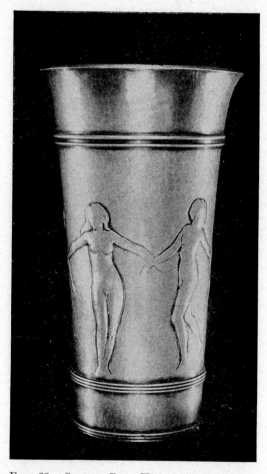

FIG. 88. SILVER CUP, HAMMERED UP FROM
CIRCULAR SHEET. IN PROCESS OF BEING CHASED.
BY AUTHOR

FIG. 89.   CHILD'S DRINKING CUP, DESIGNED
AND CHASED BY AUTHOR

CHAPTER VII

WIRE-DRAWING AND WIRE WORK

51. The process of wire-drawing has been known from the earliest time. The book of Exodus in the Old Testa-

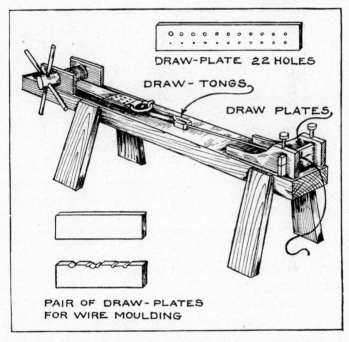

FIG. 90. THE DRAW-BENCH, USED FOR DRAWING HEAVY GAGE WIRE OR MOULDED WIRE

ment mentions the fact. As so many thousands of articles are manufactured from wire in this day and age, it is interesting and very important as well as educational to know how wire is drawn.

Some metals are more ductile than others; for that reason some can be drawn into almost inconceivable fineness and others not. It is said one ounce of gold wire can be drawn into a wire twelve miles long. Wire that fine is used in embroidery, on uniforms, and for filigree work where it is twisted and arranged in intricate patterns and de-

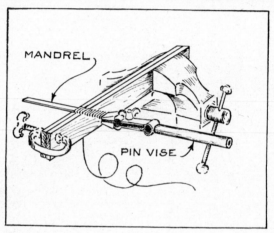

Fig. 91. Making Links for Chain Work

signs. In the manufacture of chains and jewelry, wire is most important.

52. **Draw-Plates** are of many kinds: some have round holes; others square, rectangular, half-round, hexagonal, star-shaped, etc. The draw-plate is a steel plate with a series of holes graduated in size, through which, successively, the wire is drawn. (Fig. 17) A heavy pair of pliers or "draw-tongs" are important in order to get a good grip on the pointed end of the wire. If heavy-gage wire is to be reduced, an apparatus called a draw-bench

is used. (Fig. 90) Anneal frequently as each drawing naturally hardens and compresses the metal. Light-gage wire may be pulled by hand, by placing the draw-plate in a bench vise, the principle of the operation being

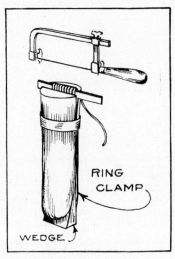

FIG. 92. SAWING THE COILED
WIRE LINKS

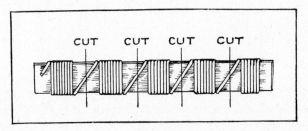

FIG. 93. WIRE WOUND ROUND MANDREL READY FOR
CUTTING

the same. By doubling up a piece of round wire and pulling it through hole after hole, it will gradually become half-round in shape. In order to avoid any risk of melting the wire when annealing, coil it up in a close bundle (Fig. 18), tie all the strands together with iron binding wire so that it forms a compact ring, and let a soft flame play on

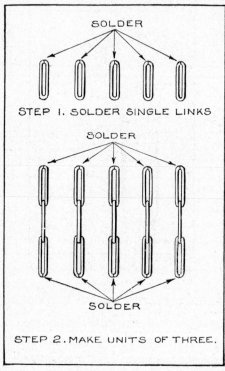

Fig. 94.   The Making of a Chain

it until it shows a uniform faint redness. It is then soft and pliable.

53. **Chain Making** is a highly important branch of the craftworker's art. To make a simple chain, such as is shown in the various pendants, is good practice work for beginners as it gives good practice in soldering, and not

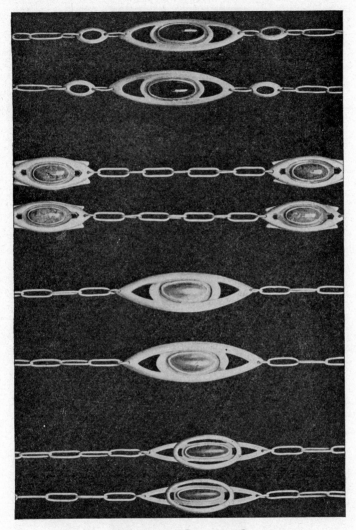

FIG. 95. CHAINS WITH INSERTED ORNAMENTS
By students of Milwaukee Downer College, Wisconsin

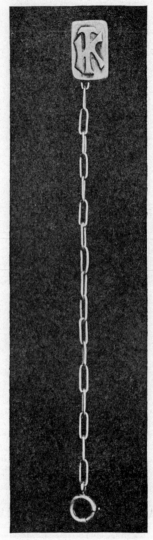

FIG. 96.   LAPEL WATCH
CHAIN

FIG. 97. JEWELRY MADE OF WIRE
UNITS

much is spoiled if a few links are burned or melted. Good

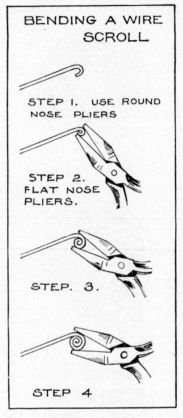

BENDING A WIRE SCROLL

STEP 1. USE ROUND NOSE PLIERS

STEP 2. FLAT NOSE PLIERS.

STEP. 3.

STEP 4

FIG. 98. HOW TO MAKE A WIRE
SPIRAL

clean soldering can be learned only through repeated practice. Chain or link work offers such an opportunity.

Tools necessary for link work are two pairs of flat-nose
pliers, a pair of round-nose pliers, tweezers, and mandrels
to wind the wire on.

Supposing a chain with oval links is to be made, similar to that on the pendant in Fig. 65, first decide on the length of the links, say ⅜-inch long, then take a piece of flat metal (copper or brass will do) and cut a strip carefully to the required width, filing the edges round and smooth, and finish with emery cloth. This is to serve as a mandrel

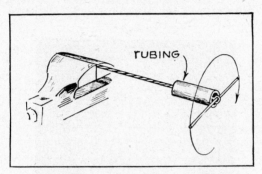

FIG. 99. TWISTING A PIECE OF WIRE

and its size will determine the size of the links. Wrap a strip of thin paper in a spiral fashion around the mandrel; tie the paper to the mandrel at each end with a piece of binding wire. The links must now be wound or coiled around the mandrel very closely and regularly; the method shown in Fig. 91 insures a good job. Heat the whole thing with the blowpipe; this will burn the paper away and make the links soft and pliable. The mandrel can now be withdrawn with ease, which otherwise would be impossible had the paper not been used. The coil is now cut lengthwise with a No. 00 jeweler's saw keeping the cut as clean as possible. (Fig. 92) The shape of the mandrel of course determines the shape of the links. Another method of coiling links without the use of paper is to wind the wire in sections of about a dozen each, as in Fig. 93, then anneal and cut the mandrel at each section and saw the links while they are still on the mandrel. This however, will destroy the mandrel, while in the first method the mandrel can be used over and over again. Each link must now be carefully joined with the two flat-nosed pliers; there must be contact where the two ends meet in order to avoid trouble when soldering. Place

FIG. 100. FILIGREE BROOCH MADE IN
ICELAND

several single links on the charcoal block and solder with a pointed flame. Now connect two links to the one just soldered and make units of three. By this method, multiple work is performed and the work is reduced to a marked degree. (Fig. 94) The chain should be tested for any weak links by a firm pull, or it may be drawn through a hole or two of the draw-plate. Now boil it out in the pickle, which will dissolve all excess borax. Chains, such as in Fig. 95, with inserted ornaments are attractive and always stimulate interest in the craft. Many variations are possible by breaking it up into units and alternating short and long links or grouping them in a pleasing man-

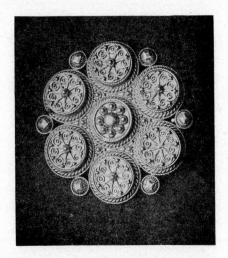

FIG. 101. FILIGREE BROOCH MADE IN NORWAY

ner. A lapel watch chain with a small ornament for the buttonhole (Fig. 96) makes a winning problem to work out with a minimum amount of work connected with it.

54. **Unit Jewelry.** The designs in Fig. 97 explain what is meant by unit work. It is well within the craftsman's reach. It is all made by bending or twisting wire into units of the same shape or form and arranging these separate pieces or units so as to produce a pleasing design. Scrolls (Fig. 98) are made by giving the end of wire a preliminary twist with a pair of round-nose pliers, after that it is squeezed gently little by little with the flat-nose pliers.

The position and grip of the pliers must be very slightly varied. Do not exert too much pressure at first or the wire will kink instead of curl. It requires a great deal of practice to make nice closed scrolls perfectly.

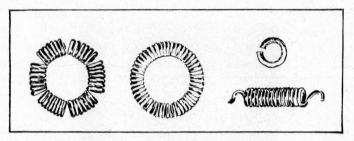

FIG. 102. WIRE COILED UP

55. Twisting Wires. Double up a piece of wire, fasten the ends in a vise, insert a piece of tubing, and twist by placing a nail in the looped end of wire. Hold the tube with one hand and twist with the other. (Fig. 99)

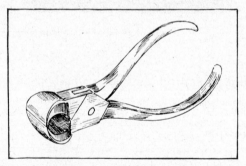

FIG. 103. THE CUTTING PLIERS

56. Filigree. The brooches in Figs. 100 and 101 are made up of many units. They may be said to consist of curling, twisting, and plaiting fine pliable threads of metal and uniting them at their points of contact with each other. Small grains or beads of metal are often set in the eyes of scrolls or at intervals to set off the wire work effectively. This type of work is called "filigree" and is characteristic of the Scandinavian countries and Iceland. However, the art was practiced by the Egyptian jewelers and the Byzantine goldsmiths. Exquisite specimens of this kind of work, made centuries ago, may be viewed in most museums. It requires a somewhat special method to solder on the many separate units to the base. Melt the borax to a glaze in a crucible or in a hollow depression in the charcoal block. Grind this borax glaze to a fine powder in a druggist's mortar with the pestle. Now with a fine file reduce a piece of solder to filings and mix equally with borax powder. This mixture should be applied along the joints to be soldered. Wherever possible apply the heat from the under side of the work; this will minimize the possibilities of displacing any of the parts to be soldered.

CHAPTER VIII

STONES AND METALS—SOLDERING

57. **Stones.** The art of cutting and polishing stones is practiced by the "lapidary." There is little difference in the instruments used by the modern lapidary and those used by the early gem cutters, but great improvements have been made in shaping and forming the stones to get the utmost beauty from the rough gem. (Fig. 104)

The rough stone is first put through the process known as slitting. This is accomplished by holding it next to a thin metal wheel which revolves at a high rate of speed and is moistened with diamond dust and oil which give it the biting edge. The discs or wheels vary in diameter from that of a pin-head to a quarter of an inch. The diamond dust and oil will carve any stone softer than a diamond itself with comparative ease. If facets are to be cut the stone is mounted with cement on the end of a small stick of wood and held against a horizontally revolving wheel. A little device called a "jamb peg" is used by the cutter to get the desired angle to the stone. The dull and colorless gem must now be polished to bring out its color and brilliancy.

The wheels or discs used in polishing are very much like those used in cutting, but instead of using an abrasive, a polishing compound such as tripoli, a decomposed limestone, or putty powder is used. The discs used to cut and polish faceted stones are made of metal, such as copper, brass, iron, or tin. Opaque or translucent stones, such as opals, moonstones, and turquoise, are usually cut cabo-

110

chon shape, that is, smoothly rounded, and polished on felt, leather, or wooden wheels or drums. Transparent gems are almost always cut with facets on account of the fine effect in producing brilliancy by reflection of light from the under side of the gem.

58. Precious Stones. The diamonds, rubies, emeralds, and sapphires are classed as the most precious of stones. The pearl is often spoken of as such but strictly speaking it is not a stone at all. Nevertheless, it is very costly when it is of high luster and quality.

59. Semi-precious Stones. The craftworker as a rule is more concerned about what are known as semi-precious stones as they give him a wide field to select from and are more appropriate for the type of work he is interested in. They offer a great variety of colors to choose from. Stones most applicable for the artist craftworker are:

[1]*Amethyst.* A purple stone of transparent crystal quartz. It looks well cut either cabochon or faceted. Hardness 7.

Aquamarine. A stone that has the color of the sea, from pale blue to sea green. It is a sister of the emerald and belongs to the beryl family. Hardness $7\frac{1}{2}$.

Azurite. A beautiful blue stone. It derives its color from the presence of copper. Hardness 4 to 5.

Bloodstone. An opaque, dark green with spots of red. Hardness $6\frac{1}{2}$.

Chalcedony. As a pure mineral it is transparent gray, often tinged with blue and green. Hardness $6\frac{1}{2}$ to 7.

Chrysoprase. This is a beautiful apple-green. The color is due to about one per cent nickel oxide. Fine specimens resemble emeralds. Hardness 7.

Coral. Ranges in color from bright pink to dark red. It is cut cabochon and makes up well with silver or gold. Hardness 5.

Jade. The best sage-green jades come from Upper Burma, British India. The darker green variety is found in New Zealand. Hardness $6\frac{1}{2}$ to 7.

[1]By courtesy of Espositer, Varni Co., New York.

Labradorite. A variety of feldspar first found in Labrador, it sparkles in many colors when turned to the light. Otherwise it has a gray, brownish appearance. Hardness 6.

Lapis Lazuli. A most beautiful opaque, azure-blue stone frequently marked with white spots of iron pyrites. It is found in Russia. Another variety of a lighter blue is found in Chili. Hardness 6.

Malachite. This green carbonate of copper (a form of copper ore) appears in layers. It is a rather soft stone but it takes a high polish. Hardness 4 to 5.

Malachite-Azurite. This is a combination of malachite and azurite, mixed to form exquisite peacock colors. Hardness 4 to 5.

Moonstone. A subvariety of feldspar. It reflects a bluish light. Hardness 6.

Moss Agate. Moss agate contains particles of iron oxide, which give it the appearance of containing vegetable matter. Hardness 6½.

Opal Matrix. This is an intermixture of opal and the rock in which it is found. The light and the dark opal matrix are used to a great extent in artistic jewelry. Hardness 6.

Turmaline. A transparent stone found in many colors, red and green predominating. Hardness 7 to 7½.

Turquoise Matrix. For art jewelry this stone is very effective. The contrast between the blue turquoise and the rock in which it is found makes it exceedingly interesting. Hardness 6.

60. Hardness. Different stones have different degrees of hardness. The hardness of gems has been expressed by the Moks[1] scale, from one to ten:

1	Talc	6	Feldspar
2	Gypsum	7	Quartz
3	Calcite	8	Topaz
4	Fluorite	9	Ruby or Sapphire
5	Apatite	10	Diamond

To find the hardness of a stone one must find what other stone of known hardness scratches it and is scratched by it.

[1] An eminent German mineralogist.

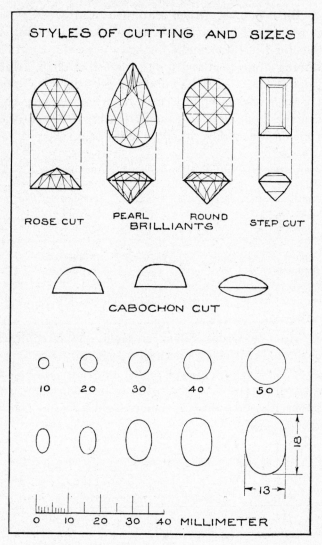

FIG. 104. HOW STONES ARE CUT AND MEASURED

61. Birth Stones. Much sentiment is attached to the language of birth stones all over the world. It is an ancient custom for friends to make birthday presents of articles containing stones representing the month of birth. Many consider them as sacred symbols or good luck. Various lists of the stones peculiar to each month of the year have been given from time to time in the last few centuries. The one most generally accepted today is as follows:

January	Garnet
February	Amethyst
March	Bloodstone
April	Sapphire or Diamond
May	Emerald
June	Agate
July	Ruby
August	Sardonyx
September	Chrysolite
October	Opal
November	Topaz
December	Turquoise

62. How to Order Silver or Gold. When ordering silver or gold it is always necessary to specify what make of gage. Browne and Sharpe is well known by all dealers. Sterling silver and fine silver, the latter sometimes used for bezels, is sold by the troy ounce. Gold is sold by pennyweight (dwt.).

24 grains = 1 pennyweight (dwt.)
20 pennyweights = 1 ounce (oz.)
12 ounces = 1 pound (lb.)

The following table shows the approximate cost per square inch of sterling silver, 14 and 18 carat gold, based on present current prices of 90 cents per ounce of sterling silver and 70 cents per dwt. of 14 carat gold plate and 88 cents per dwt. for 18 carat gold plate.

Gage	Sterling silver	14 carat gold	18 carat gold
8	.65	14.08	18.10
9	.58	12.61	16.23
10	.46	11.20	14.44
11	.41	10.01	12.91
12	.36	8.93	11.48
13	.35	8.18	10.19
14	.32	7.06	9.26
15	.28	6.32	8.06
16	.25	5.61	7.22
17	.22	4.97	6.38
18	.20	4.40	5.68
19	.18	3.99	5.09
20	.17	3.56	4.54
21	.14	3.04	3.92
22	.13	2.77	3.52
23	.12	2.47	3.19
24	.11	2.21	2.86
26	.08	1.76	2.28
28	.07	1.32	1.73
30	.05	1.05	1.43

Sterling silver can be purchased cut in circular shape. The weight of a silver circle is $78\frac{27}{50}$ per cent of the weight of a square of the same size as the circle's diameter.

TABLE SHOWING NUMBER OF FEET OF STERLING SILVER WIRE PER TROY OUNCE

Wire can be purchased round- or square-drawn

Gage	Feet	Inches	Gage	Feet	Inches
8	1	2	18	11	10
9	1	6	19	14	9
10	1	10	20	18	5
11	2	4	21	24	4
12	2	11	22	30	6
13	3	8	23	39	6
14	4	7	24	47	9
15	5	11	26	74	7
16	7	4	28	132	5
17	9	5	30	191	0

TABLE OF WEIGHTS PER SQUARE FOOT OF COPPER AND BRASS

B.&.S gage	B.&S. thickness in decimal	Brass per lb.	Copper per lb.
10	.102	4.36	4.62
11	.091	3.88	4.11
12	.081	3.46	3.66
13	.072	3.08	3.26
14	.064	2.74	2.90
15	.057	2.44	2.58
16	.051	2.18	2.30
17	.045	1.94	2.05
18	.040	1.72	1.82
19	.036	1.54	1.63
20	.032	1.37	1.45
21	.028	1.22	1.29
22	.025	1.08	1.15
23	.022	.97	1.02
24	.020	.86	.91
25	.018	.77	.81
26	.016	.68	.72
27	.014	.61	.64
28	.012	.54	.57
29	.011	.48	.51
30	.010	.43	.45

63. Melting Silver and Scraps. It is often desirable to melt small quantities of scrap silver. This can easily be done as there are excellent small crucible furnaces on the market, costing about three dollars. (Fig. 105) The silver scraps are placed in the open crucible furnace with a small amount of borax or flux, the gas is turned on and the foot blower set in action. When the metal is properly melted, which requires only a few minutes, the silver is poured into an ingot (Fig. 106) or mold. It is necessary to warm and grease the ingot beforehand to prevent the silver from spitting and sticking to its sides.

64. **Rolling.** When the silver has been cast into a small bar it must be rolled to the desired thickness or gage. This is done by passing it through a pair of steel rolls (Fig. 107) working very much on the same principle as a wringer used in washing. After each passage through the rollers the metal is flattened little by little. Frequent annealing must be resorted to so as to counteract the hardening caused by pressure of the rollers.

EASY-FLOWING SOLDER: 90 parts sterling silver
                            6 parts copper
                            4 parts zinc
HARD-FLOWING SOLDER: 90 parts sterling silver
                            8 parts copper
                            2 parts zinc
EASY-FLOWING: Fine silver, 1 oz.
                      Pure copper, 5 dwts.
                      Composition metal, 5 dwts.
HARD-FLOWING: Fine silver, 1 oz.
                      Brass, 10 dwts.

Melt the silver in a small crucible first, adding a small amount of borax as flux. When in a molten state the brass and composition metal is added and the crucible given a gentle shake to mix the alloy, or an iron rod may be used for stirring. Then pour the metal into an ingot or mold.

65. **Composition Metal** is an alloy. It is composed of a mixture of copper and spelter. A good grade of brass should be used, such as brass escutcheon pins or nails or screws of brass. The copper must be of the purest; electro-deposited copper is best as it is practically 100 per cent pure. Silver solder, however, can be purchased from jewelers or refiners in small quantities, both hard- and easy-flowing.

66. **Soft Solder.** The strength of a soldered joint depends upon the strength of the solder used. Solders are

classed as hard and soft solders. The former always requires a red-hot heat. The latter, soft solder or tin solder, is used for many different purposes where the soldered articles need not be heated much above the boiling point of water. It is used primarily by sheet-metal workers and tinsmiths. The jewelers and silver-smiths use it at times but very rarely.

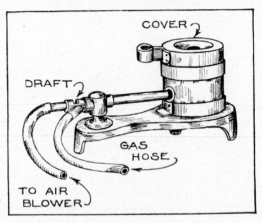

Fig. 105. The Crucible Furnace for Melt-ing Scraps or Small Quantities of Metals

The solder commercially known as "half-and-half" (50–50 tin and lead) answers the purpose for most general work. The parts to be joined must be thoroughly cleaned and free from oxide. The edges to be soldered must fit or be in contact with each other.

67. **Flux for Soft Solder.** To prevent a layer of oxide from forming on the metal in the process of heating, a so-called "flux" is used. The flux is applied to the joint, partly to keep off the air, thus preventing oxidation, and partly to dissolve and reduce the oxides themselves.

Many preparations are on the market as flux in soft-soldering, such as zinc chloride, tallow, resin, sal ammoniac, and soldering paste. The zinc chloride is old and reliable. It is prepared by adding zinc cuttings to muriatic acid or hydrochloric acid. Let stand until it has finished

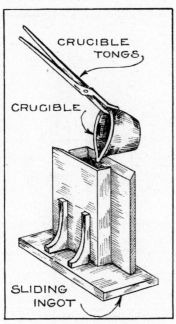

FIG. 106. POURING THE MOULTEN
METAL INTO THE INGOT

boiling, then strain off into a bottle for future use. A small piece of sal ammoniac added to the strained fluid will improve it as a flux.

68. Soldering Iron or Bit. Tinsmiths or sheet-metal workers use this tool almost entirely in performing their soldering jobs. It is made of copper in various weights and shapes. A small copper becomes cool quickly with poor work as a result. It is advisable to use a good-sized copper bit as it will sustain the heat longer. The bit shown in Fig. 108, *A*, is filed or forged to a point and well adapted for spotting or soldering a seam. The bottom copper (Fig. 108, *B*) is wedge-shaped and used for solder-

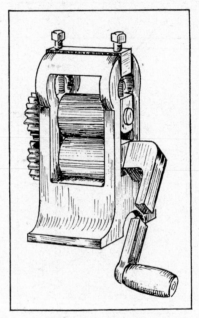

FIG. 107. THE ROLLING MILL

ing on the inside of an article. This shape also adapts itself well for radio work.

69. **Tinning Copper Point.** A bit must be tinned on the point before it is ready for use. Heat the copper sufficiently to melt the solder. With an old rough file clean the sides, then rub it on a lump of sal ammoniac. A small piece of solder is now melted on the sal ammoniac block,

and the bit is rubbed again back and forth. This process will tin the point; then it is ready for use. The point of the soldering bit must be kept clean and bright at all

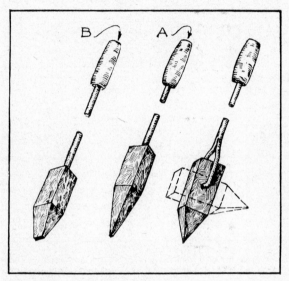

FIG. 108. THE SOLDERING COPPER, USED ONLY
IN SOFT SOLDERING

times. The copper oxide or scale which forms during the heating process is nearly a nonconductor of heat and renders the bit practically useless. If the bit has been overheated, that is, if it has been allowed to become red-hot, then it must be retinned.

70. **Cleaning the Bit by Dipping.** The point of the hot soldering iron may be cleaned by dipping it quickly in a solution made from $\frac{1}{4}$ of an ounce of sal ammoniac dissolved in a pint of water. The object in using the soldering

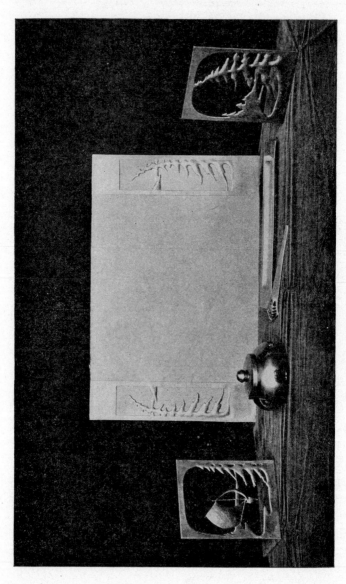

FIG. 109. DESK SET WITH BOOK ENDS
Made by students of Milwaukee Downer College, Wisconsin

copper is to transmit the heat from the bit to the work as quickly as possible. By raising the temperature of the soldering copper and the part to be soldered, the fusing together of parts is almost instantaneous.

CHAPTER IX

HAMMERED WORK

71. **The Work Described** in the pages to follow will deal with what is commonly known as "art metalwork." This term, however, comprises such a wide range of different kinds of work and processes that it may be well to keep within a certain limit. Many attractive pieces of work may be executed with only a minimum amount of labor spent and at the same time have distinct educational value. It is fascinating and interesting to watch the many forms a piece of silver, copper, or brass takes as it gradually yields to the blows of the hammer. Thin, flimsy metalwork should be avoided; it is not substantial and is easily dented.

72. **Flat Work.** The bookends in Fig. 110 are made from sheet-copper or brass, gage 16. The design should be drawn full-size and may be made to fit a given size set of books. Cut the metal with a pair of 12-inch shears.

73. **Planishing** is the process of giving the metal surface a finish with a steel planishing hammer. (Fig. 135) The metal is held firmly on a solid iron block or anvil and hammer blows are delivered uniformly with the slightly curved surface of the planishing hammer. This will result in a delightful hammered texture, provided the face of the hammer and the surface of the work are clean and free from grease and grit. It is important to hold the hammer in a level position so that the blows fall squarely on the metal. Unpleasant blemishes will result should the edge of the hammer strike the metal.

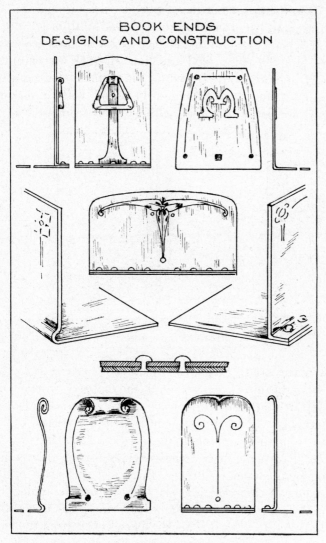

Fig. 110. Designs for Metal Book Ends

After planishing, the bookends are annealed and thrown into the diluted sulphuric-acid solution for cleaning. With a rawhide mallet the metal is flattened carefully and the edges filed and finished with emery cloth. If any lines are to be traced on the surface for decorative purposes the tracing should be done with a chasing tool (see Chapter VI) and hammered on a flat iron, or, if

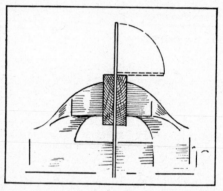

Fig. 111. Bending a Piece of Metal Held Between Two Pieces of Wood

any places are to be pierced open, the jeweler's saw must be brought into use. To bend the base of a bookend, clamp it between two pieces of wood and bend over. (Fig. 111) The bent-over piece may be struck lightly with a hammer to make the corner a little sharper.

74. Rivets may be purchased in almost any size, made from iron, copper, or brass. The size is measured by the diameter of the stem, and the length from the under side of the head to the end. The rivet has great decorative value in craft work if properly spaced. Get from the local hardware dealer an assortment of different sizes for reference purposes. Escutcheon pins can be used to good advantage as rivets. This kind of nail always has a nicely rounded head.

75. **To Rivet,** first drill the hole as nearly as possible the size of the rivet. Remove the burr with a countersink; insert the rivet and cut it with the nippers or cutting pliers so that it projects about $\frac{1}{16}$ inch which will provide

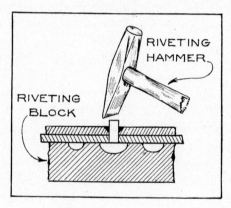

FIG. 112.   RIVETING

enough metal for riveting. A piece of iron which has cup-shaped depressions of different sizes on the surface is necessary for good work. This will form a bed for the round head of the rivet and prevent flattening of the head of the rivet. (Fig. 112) The riveting hammer will spread the rivet and clinch the parts together.

76. **Letter Opener.** A project of this kind works up well by combining copper and brass. The knives shown in Fig. 113 are made of brass and copper. Cut the blade from 15 gage brass with a jeweler's saw, using a No. 1 saw blade, and file sharp but blunt. The applied metal for the handle part is cut from 20 gage copper and riveted on with brass rivets or escutcheon pins.

77. Drawer Pulls. Metalwork for surface enrichment gives the craftworker a large field to explore by studying the many period furniture trimmings to be seen in any good furniture store. The drawer pulls in Fig. 114 are composed of three parts—the plate, the pull, and the strap. The design must be made full-size always, then transferred to the metal by one of the processes previously explained. Use metal of an 18 gage for the plate and saw out with a jeweler's saw. If a hammered effect is desired, then the metal must be planished before it is sawed out, otherwise the edges will be damaged and the plate thrown out of shape. The pull is made from heavy-gage wire, No. 1 or No. 2. This wire may be hammered or forged into whatever form is desired. If the work is in copper or iron, it should be hammered red-hot; if made from brass, anneal it frequently, but hammer it while cold as it is liable to crack or split, being an alloyed metal. The pull may be fastened to the plate by any of the methods shown in Fig. 115. The straps at *A* and *B* should be made from 22 gage metal. The bolt at *C* is filed and riveted on to the plate. The method at *D* can be made by soldering a brass nut on the back of the plate with a machine screw to fit. This last method is the most common way of fastening metal trimmings to furniture. The drawer or door pulls in Figs. 116 and 117 were made in copper, and rivets used as a part of the decorative scheme. Metal trimmings applicable to furniture are shown in Figs. 118 and 119.

78. The Dapping Die and tools (Fig. 120) are used to make half-spheres of smaller sizes, which can be used for feet of a tray or shallow bowl, or for decorative purposes to take the place of rivets. Cut a small circular disc from metal of any gage and place it in the largest cavity of the

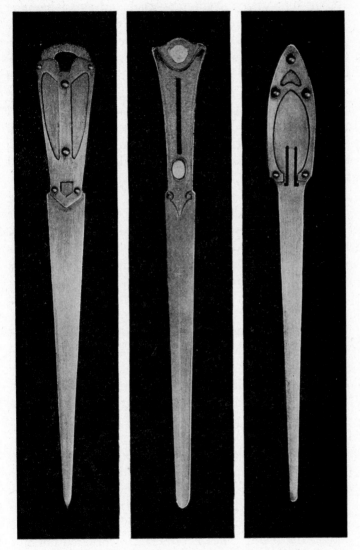

Fig. 113. Letter Openers, Copper and Brass

dapping die; with the dapping tool and small hammer form it to the shape of the cavity. Now place it in the next size smaller cavity of the die and repeat the operation, and so on. In this manner the circular disc gradually takes the shape of half a sphere. Two can be soldered together to make a whole sphere. Some fitting and filing of course is necessary before the two halves are tied together with iron binding wire for soldering. A small vent hole must be drilled somewhere, previous to soldering; otherwise, in successive heating of the ball the imprisoned gases would expand, and the ball would explode.

79. Lanterns. Lanterns such as the one shown in Fig. 121 may be used as light fixtures for a porch, or a pair of lanterns may appropriately be used above a fireplace where a mellow subdued light is desired. Stained glass or amber-colored mica (isinglass) are both suitable mediums for covering the open or pierced design. Isinglass is a silicate that cleaves in thin, tough, transparent to translucent scales.

To make the lantern, develop the parts marked *A* and *B* on a heavy manila paper; cut out the pattern, score the bending lines and fold to the shape of the drawing. By doing this it is possible to see what the finished work will look like, and you can also better judge the proportions.

Now transfer the patterns *A* and *B* to a piece of copper, 24 gage; cut as much as is practical with the shears, then saw out the rest with a jeweler's saw. Centerpunch places where the rivets are to go, then drill holes a trifle larger than the neck of the rivet. The work must now be cleaned in the pickle and flattened carefully with the rawhide mallet on a level piece of wood or on an iron surface plate. To bend the metal, place it on a sharp-cornered piece of wood or iron and turn it over to the proper angle. The

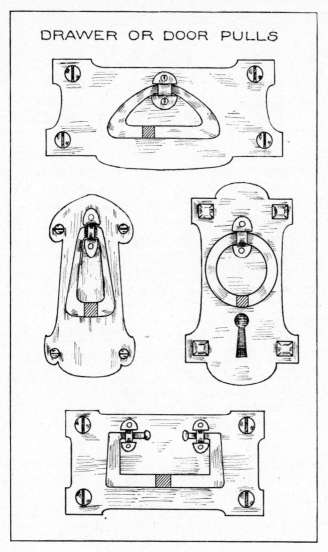

FIG. 114.   DESIGNS FOR DRAWER AND DOOR PULLS

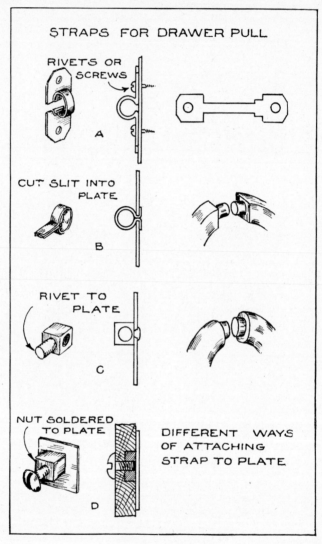

FIG. 115. DIFFERENT METHODS OF FASTENING PULL TO DRAWER PLATE

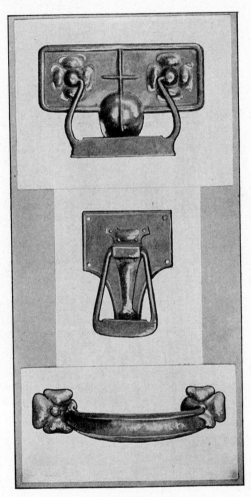

FIG. 116. DRAWER PULLS
By Mr. G. H. Trautman

joints should be filed and fitted accurately and soft-soldered. To make the joint strong and secure, reinforce by placing an angle piece on the inside (Fig. 122) and solder by holding it over the gas or alcohol flame.

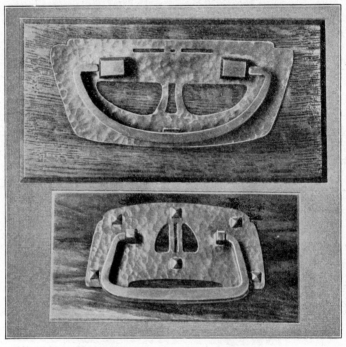

FIG. 117.   COPPER DRAWER PULLS

The rivets are placed as a part of the decorative scheme and serve only as such.

The **Z**-shaped pieces of metal to hold the glass in place are made from a light-gage metal, about 28, and soft-soldered in place.

The base plate is made from 18 gage metal with hole and slots as shown.

The lower receptacle for candle or electric light socket must be made from metal of the same gage as the base plate and domed up in a hollow depression on a wood

Fig. 118. Waste Paper Basket
with Applied Metal Work

block with the ball-pein hammer, (Fig. 122, *D*) after which it must be planished in order to give it a smooth and finished appearance. Clinch the ball-pein hammer in the vise and strike even, gentle blows with a planishing hammer, starting at the center and working round and round toward the edge. By doing this the work will take a perfect round shape.

The bracket may be made from 18 or 16 gage copper

Fig. 119. Writing Desk with Applied Metal Work

sawed to shape with a No. 1 or 2 saw blade. It is always advisable to use a coarse saw blade when cutting heavy-gage metal.

The supporting chain is made of 10 gage wire. Coil it around a mandrel of suitable size to form oval links. (See Sec. 53.) The supporting hook and eye is made from the same gage of wire bent to the shape as shown.

This lantern mounted on a black walnut board makes an attractive and interesting piece of work.

Figs. 123 and 124 offer two different shapes with suggestive motifs for design. The principal part of the lantern is developed or unfolded. Only operations described in the preceding problem are encountered here.

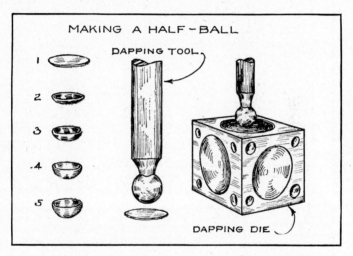

Fig. 120.   The Dapping Dies and Dapping Tools

The lantern in Fig. 125 is a riveted piece of work. Rivets of pleasing sizes should be selected and grouped. The six upright supporting members are each bent to form an angle of 120 degrees. The upper dome should be raised to a height of about $1\frac{1}{2}$ inches in a depression on a block of wood or a log, with a ball-pein hammer, and afterwards planished. To give this lantern a wrought or hammered appearance the metal must be hammered with a slightly curved planishing hammer on a level piece of iron, before it is cut to accurate pattern shape.

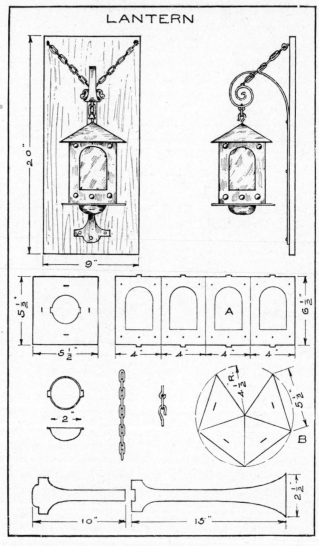

FIG. 121. WALL LANTERN WITH WORKING DRAWINGS

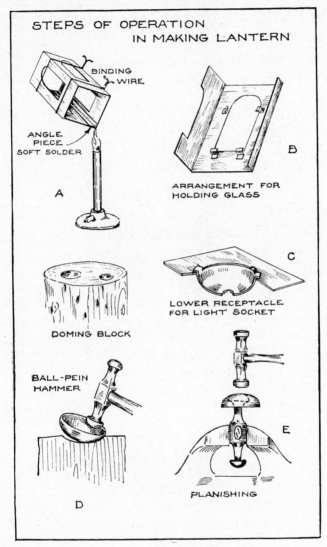

STEPS OF OPERATION
IN MAKING LANTERN

BINDING WIRE

ANGLE PIECE
SOFT SOLDER

A

B

ARRANGEMENT FOR
HOLDING GLASS

C

LOWER RECEPTACLE
FOR LIGHT SOCKET

DOMING BLOCK

BALL-PEIN
HAMMER

D

E

PLANISHING

Fig. 122. Important Steps in Making Wall Lantern

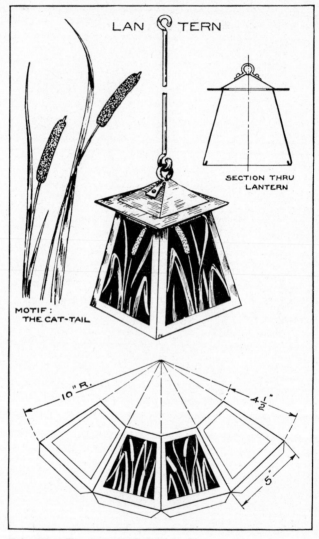

FIG. 123. TRUNCATED PYRAMID SHAPED LANTERN WITH
MOTIF FOR THE DESIGN

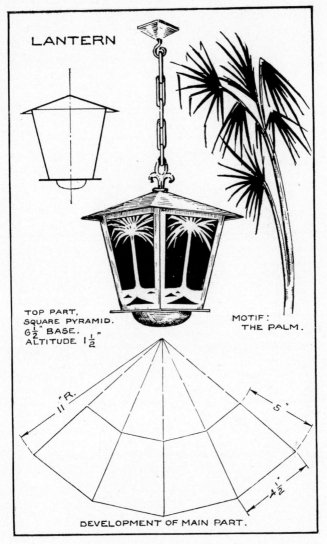

LANTERN

TOP PART,
SQUARE PYRAMID.
$6\frac{1}{2}$" BASE.
ALTITUDE $1\frac{1}{2}$"

MOTIF:
THE PALM.

11" R.

5"

$4\frac{1}{2}$"

DEVELOPMENT OF MAIN PART.

FIG. 124. CEILING LANTERN, INVERTED PYRAMID SHAPE,
WITH MOTIF FOR DESIGN

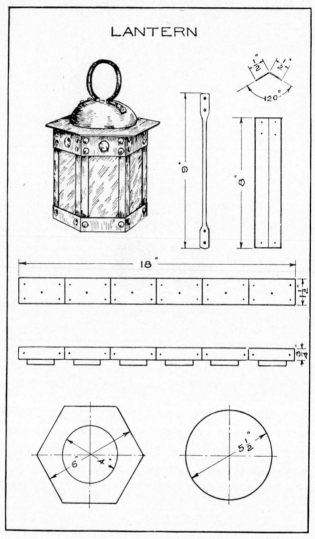

FIG. 125.   RIVETED LANTERN, HEXAGONAL SHAPED

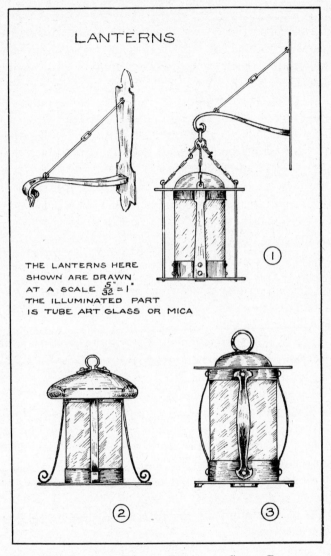

LANTERNS

THE LANTERNS HERE
SHOWN ARE DRAWN
AT A SCALE $\frac{5"}{32} = 1"$
THE ILLUMINATED PART
IS TUBE ART GLASS OR MICA

FIG. 126. LANTERN DESIGNS DRAWN TO SCALE, PROBLEMS
TO BE WORKED OUT IN DETAILS

This latter process will cause the metal to become hard and unwieldy. To render it soft and pliable again it is necessary to anneal it and clean it in the sulphuric-acid pickle solution, then straighten it carefully with a rawhide mallet on a smooth, flat piece of wood or iron.

The three lanterns in Fig. 126 are problems to be worked out in detail. The illuminated part is cylindrical tubing of art glass or mica which may be purchased in many various shades and colors, and diameters cut to any length. (See list of Dealers.)

Amber-colored mica gives a pleasing, mellow light and may be used to good advantage also. The drawing is made to the scale stated. Measurements may be obtained by scaling the drawing or they may be approximated.

80. **Desk Set.** For the type of corners on the blotter support shown in Fig. 128 it is well to make an exact development on heavy drawing paper. (Fig. 129) Score the folding line, then cut the outline and fold together. This will serve as a pattern for final marking.

Cut from soft sheet-copper, 24 gage, four pieces a little larger than the pattern. Select the better side of the metal for the top side of the work and planish with the curved end of the planishing hammer on a smooth, flat iron. This will result in a pleasing texture to the surface, but it also hardens the metal to a considerable degree. Anneal to restore ductility and clean the metal in acid pickle solution, then straighten with rawhide mallet.

Lay out the paper pattern on each piece of metal and scribe carefully around it, marking all corners to be bent. With a pair of snips cut out each piece; if necessary use the jeweler's saw.

To bend the corners, square up a piece of hardwood ¼ inch thick. Place the metal accurately on the line and,

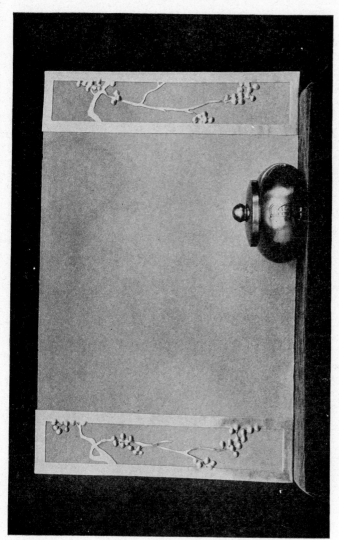

FIG. 127. DESK SET. INKWELL AND BLOTTER SUPPORT, BITTER-SWEET DESIGN
Students' work, Milwaukee Downer College, Wisconsin

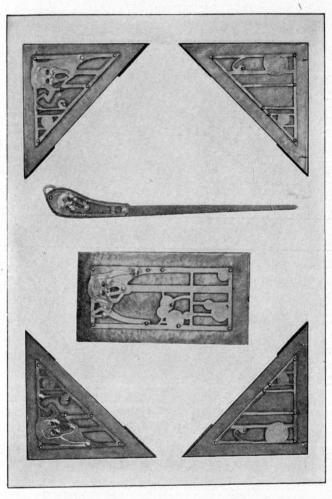

Fig. 128. Desk Set with Corners for Blotter Support. Rocking Blotter and Letter Opener. Made of Copper and Brass

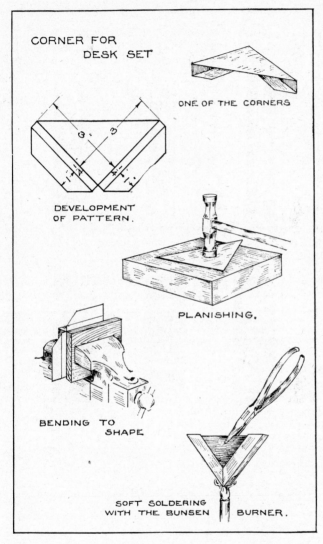

CORNER FOR DESK SET

ONE OF THE CORNERS

DEVELOPMENT OF PATTERN.

PLANISHING.

BENDING TO SHAPE

SOFT SOLDERING WITH THE BUNSEN BURNER.

Fig. 129. Making the Corners for a Desk Set

FIG. 130. DESIGNS AND CONSTRUCTION OF DESK PAD SUPPORT

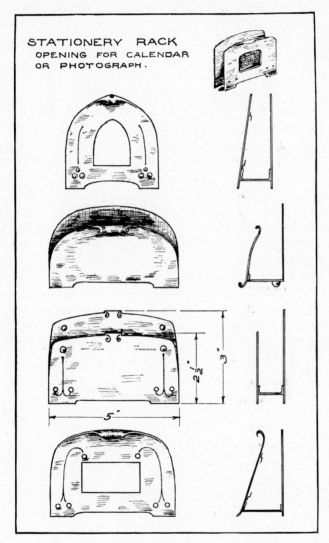

FIG. 131. STATIONERY RACK FOR DESK SET

with a scrap piece of wood as backing, squeeze in the vise while the metal is bent over the ¼-inch wood as shown. A drop of soft solder placed on the inside will seal the joint. Another type of pad is shown in Fig. 130.

The designs with all dimensions for the letter rack (Fig. 131) are suggestions for further study. The rivets may be placed to answer a double purpose, as part of the construction and as a decorative medium, if they are properly spaced and suitable sizes are chosen.

Use an 18 gage metal for upright members and 22 for inside work. The **Z**-shaped piece for holding the calendar pad may be made of a lighter gage metal.

CHAPTER X

Raised Work

81. **Shallow Bowls or Trays.** The essential equipment
for raised work consists of a log 2 feet high and about 12
inches in diameter, hammers and stakes of various shapes
and sizes. The object is to hammer up from a flat sheet
of metal any desired shape.

If a round tray similar to any of the ones shown in Fig.
132 is to be made, the first thing to decide upon is the
diameter of the circular disc from which the work is to
be made. Several methods are employed. One fairly
accurate method for the beginner is to measure the length
of the contour by a string or a piece of wire, as $A–B–C–D$
in Fig. 132. Another common method is to take the
straight line distance, as shown by the dotted line $A–B–C–$
D. Finally, the experienced hammer worker takes for
his diameter the height plus the greatest diameter; this
last method, however, requires that the worker know the
ductility of the metal, as it must be stretched to a marked
degree.

The circular disc is cut with the shears from 20 gage
silver, copper, or brass. File clean around the edge; next
anneal and clean in the sulphuric-acid pickle solution,
rinse in clean water and dry. The metal disc is now held
over a shallow cavity which has been gouged out of the
end of a good-sized log, and light blows delivered uniformly with the ball-pein hammer, moving the disc a
little in a circular direction at every blow. (Fig. 133)
The edge gets wavy, and great care must be taken that no

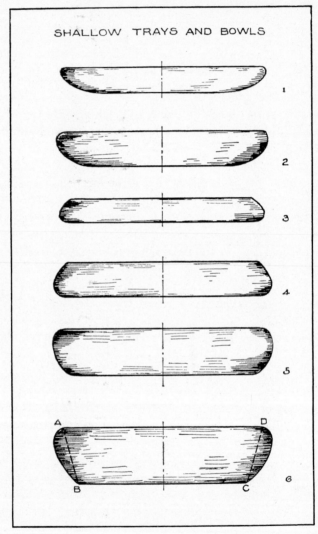

FIG. 132. SHAPES SUITABLE FOR BEGINNING WORK

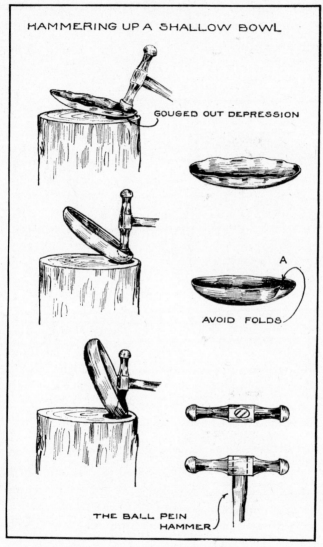

HAMMERING UP A SHALLOW BOWL

GOUGED OUT DEPRESSION

A

AVOID FOLDS

THE BALL PEIN HAMMER

FIG. 133. THE BALL PEIN HAMMER IN USE

overlap occurs (*A*, Fig. 133) which invariably results in a crack along the edge, due to the extreme stress put upon the metal at that point.

A wooden mallet or horn mallet shaped as in Fig. 134 is frequently used in place of the ball-pein hammer for

MALLETS AND DOMING LOG

WOODEN MALLET

HORN MALLET

LOG
12" DIA. 24" LONG.

Fɪɢ. 134.   Eꜱꜱᴇɴᴛɪᴀʟ Tᴏᴏʟꜱ ꜰᴏʀ ᴛʜᴇ Cʀᴀꜰᴛᴡᴏʀᴋᴇʀ

forming trays and shallow bowls. It has the advantage over the steel hammer in that the shape can easily be changed with a file or wood rasp.

The object must be annealed at the end of each round and the operation repeated until the desired form is obtained.

82. **Planishing.** Before this final process is undertaken the work should be annealed and boiled in the pickle solution, after which it is rinsed in water and dried. The object is to get it clean and free from any grease whatsoever.

Select a stake or iron suitable in shape to the outline of

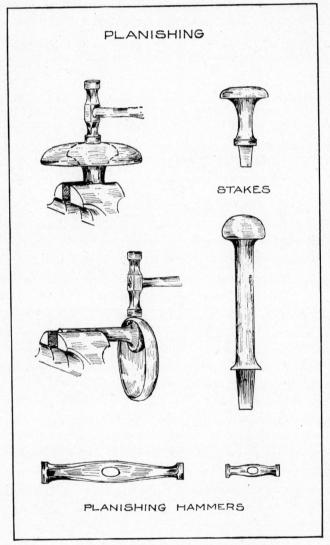

PLANISHING

STAKES

PLANISHING HAMMERS

Fig. 135. The Planishing Process

the work and planish by using a hammer with a polished face, (Fig. 135) starting in the center and working around, which can best be done if a few very light circles (not scratches) are marked on the surface with a pair of blunt-pointed dividers. This will true up the work and leave the surface bright and covered all over with brilliant

FILING AN EDGE

8 FLAT FILE
HAND SMOOTH

FIG. 136. LEVELING A PIECE OF WORK WITH A FLAT FILE

facets. It is often necessary to planish the work several times to get a perfectly smooth surface, annealing and pickling after each planishing. The somewhat irregular edge is leveled with a flat file (Fig. 136) and the sharp edge made blunt with a piece of emery cloth. To gain a perfect control of the hammer so that each blow is delivered squarely, much practice is essential.

83. Raising Hollow Vessels. The skilled craftsman can raise or draw up from a flat sheet of metal a vessel of almost any shape. It demands complete mastery of the hammer and doming mallet, and only through repeated practice can this be hoped for. Fig. 137 shows a silversmith at work on a large oval punch bowl. The design is mounted on a drawing board in front of the workman; it is being drawn up from a flat, oval piece of metal by skillful manipulation of the raising hammer and annealed regularly at the end of each beating.

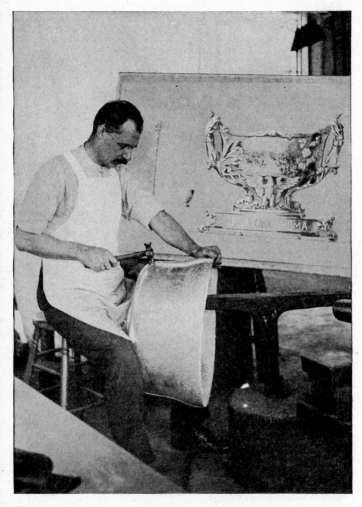

FIG. 137. SILVER PUNCH BOWL FOR U. S. BATTLESHIP "OKLA-
HOMA" IN PROCESS OF BEING RAISED

By courtesy of The Gorham Co., New York

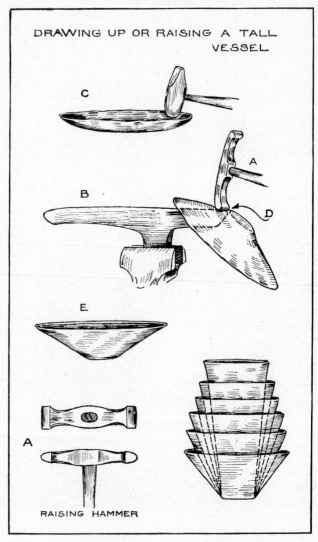

Fig. 138. Successive Steps in Raising a Vessel from a Flat Circular Sheet of Metal

This process eliminates seams and solder, and by crowding the metal together on the upper edge with the wooden mallet it is possible to increase the thickness along the rim several times its original gage.

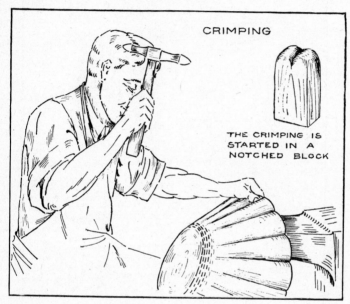

Fig. 139. Raising a Vessel Which First Has Been Crimped

Tools for this kind of work consist of the ball-pein hammer, the raising hammer (*A*, Fig. 138), the shaped mallet, and an anvil, as shown.

The cup (Fig. 88) was made in the following manner, but from a sterling silver, gage 20 B. & S., circular disc with a diameter equal to the largest diameter of the design plus one half the total height. Smooth the edge with a file and anneal the metal. Mark the bottom circle with a pair of dividers. The points of the divider must

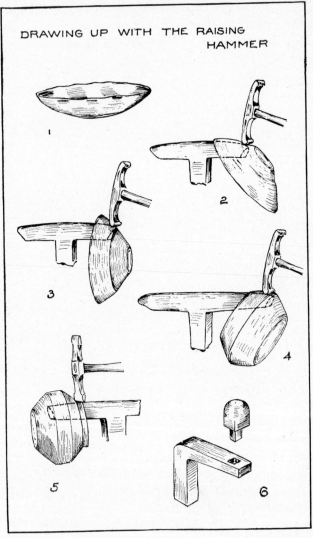

DRAWING UP WITH THE RAISING
HAMMER

Fig. 140. Successive Steps in Drawing Up a Piece of
Work

be blunt in doing this; the object is merely to provide a
light guide line for the hammer to follow.

Start by using the dome-shaped mallet, hammering
the metal carefully along the marked circle over a shallow

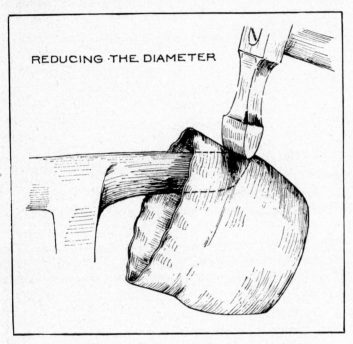

REDUCING ·THE· DIAMETER

FIG. 141.   DRAWING IN THE NECK OF A VESSEL

depression in a block of wood. The appearance will be as
in *C*, Fig. 138. Before going any further the work must
be annealed again and by throwing it into the sulphuric-
acid pickle solution after each annealing it will be clean
to handle.

The process of "raising" now begins. It is done by
placing the work against the tip of a stake so that the

edge of the stake comes close to the edge of the circle previously made. With the raising hammer beat the metal away from you, around the circle, (*D*, Fig. 138). Continue this operation, going a little higher up each round until the outer edge or top is reached, then reanneal. It will then look like *E* in Fig. 138. By repeating the last process and annealing each time, the upper edge is reached. The metal will be raised a little higher after each beating.

If working to a definite shape, a template should be made showing the exact contour of the design. When the shape of the object has been obtained the work must be planished smooth. This is performed as described in Sec. 74.

84. Crimping. This operation raises the edge. The method is used by experienced silversmiths. It is the quickest method by which a large deep piece of work can be raised without seaming. It requires a high degree of skill and much practice.

The metal is wrinkled in a notched block of wood, even and straight, with the raising hammer, then beaten down by holding the work upon the tee-stake (Fig. 139). Great care must be exercised in hammering down wrinkles that no overlap of the metal occurs, for that would result in the metal cracking.

The inkwell holder shown with the desk set (Fig. 127) may be made as shown in successive steps in Fig. 140. To reduce the diameter the work is placed on the stake as shown in Fig. 141. Naturally, by crowding in the metal the thickness along the upper edge is increased. To develop the shape and adjust the contour, work it from the inside with the ball-pein hammer, placing it on a sandbag. The planishing or surface finish should not be undertaken before the design has been realized.

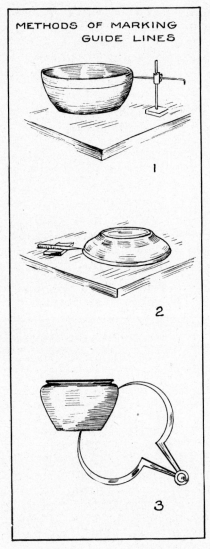

METHODS OF MARKING
GUIDE LINES

1

2

3

Fig. 142. Different Methods of
Gaging or Marking a Line

FIG. 143. COPPER TRAY
Hammered by Mr. G. H. Trautmann

The horse stake shown in the lower right corner of Fig. 140 may be fitted with a head of any shape and makes a very useful tool for planishing purposes. For describing guide use the calipers (Fig. 142) or a metalworker's surface gage.

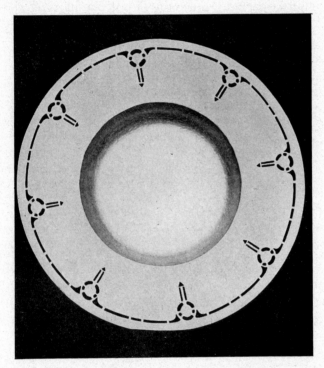

Fig. 144. Platter with Pierced Design

85. Trays and Platters. One of the most difficult things to make is a large tray or serving platter, but small ones are quite within the reach of the craftsman. A round tray (Fig. 144) should be made from a fairly substantial gage of metal, 18 or 20 B. & S.

Cut the circular-shaped disc a little larger in diameter than the desired finished plate. Describe a circle where the depression starts. The metal is placed on a flat iron and the depression beaten down with the ball-pein hammer and afterward planished carefully. (Fig. 146) For planishing a large, flat surface the face of the hammer should

FIG. 145. PEN TRAY FOR DESK SET
By G. H. Trautmann

be slightly curved. The appearance is greatly improved and strength is added to the work if the edge is reinforced with a half-round wire. (Fig. 147) Iron clamps similar to the ones shown in Fig. 25 are used. The clamps are placed at frequent spacing to insure close contact between the wire and the work proper.

86. Seaming. Tall metal objects are usually seamed; that is, a development is made, and the edges are properly jointed and hard-soldered together. This makes the seam. Assuming a vase, as in Fig. 148, is to be made, first the shape must be studied. The dotted line shows the approximate cone the design resembles. Develop a pattern by using this cone about three times in succession. Cut a piece of metal, gage 22, to the size and shape of the pat-

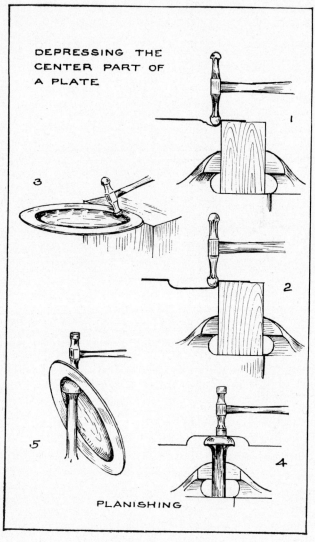

DEPRESSING THE
CENTER PART OF
A PLATE

PLANISHING

FIG. 146. SUCCESSIVE STEPS IN MAKING A PLATTER

tern and prepare the seam for soldering by filing the adjacent edges to an angle of about 45 degrees. This will give a little larger soldering surface which in turn gives a stronger joint.

Bend the metal so that the edges come together and cut a notch as at A in Fig. 148. This will act as a lock and prevent the edges from slipping by each other; the edges must fit perfectly to insure a good soldering joint. Iron

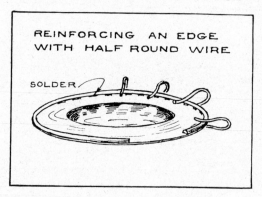

REINFORCING AN EDGE WITH HALF ROUND WIRE

SOLDER

FIG. 147. SOLDERING A WIRE EDGE ON

binding wire may be used to good advantage to hold the joint secure. The silver solder is placed on the inside in small pieces next to each other and soldered with the blow torch. Remove all fused borax and oxide by boiling in the sulphuric-acid pickle solution.

With the seam resting firmly on the stake, hammer it down to even thickness, then true it up by continued turning and hammering. File the edges clean and anneal it again.

From now on it may be treated in the same manner as if it were raised from a flat piece of metal. A bottom, of course, will have to be fitted in and soldered.

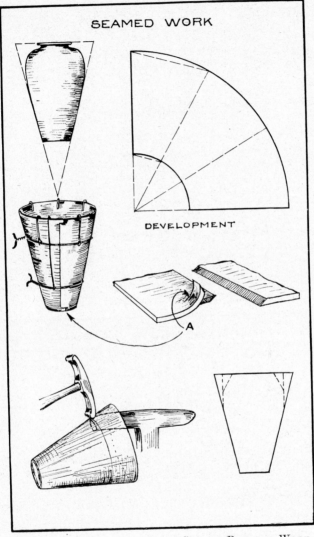

SEAMED WORK

DEVELOPMENT

A

Fig. 148. Preparations for a Seamed Piece of Work

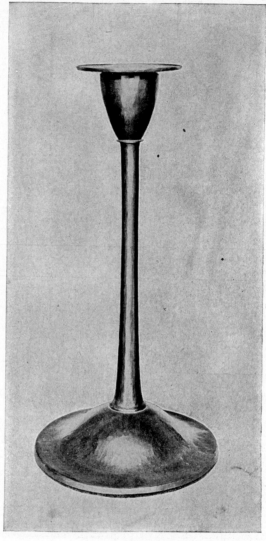

FIG. 149. HAMMERED COPPER CANDLESTICK
By G. H. Trautmann

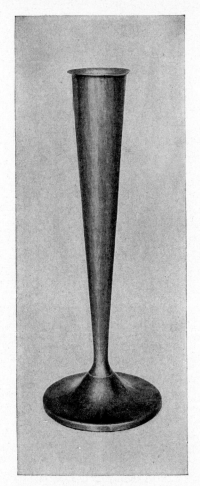

FIG. 150. HAMMERED BRASS BUD
VASE

By G. H. Trautmann

Fig. 151. Hammered Copper Candle-
HOLDER
By G. H. Trautmann

CHAPTER XI

Metal Coloring—Oxidizing

87. Metal coloring. In order to give the work a finished appearance after all the tool work is done, it is essential that it be taken through a finishing process so that the design will be brought out in its best possible form and color.

Most metals, when in a massive state, retain their brightness in dry oxygen or air, but in a moist atmosphere most of them will gradually become oxidized. For example, when a piece of iron is exposed to moisture and to the air, which contains a mixture of many gases—oxygen, nitrogen, carbonic acid, ammonia, ozone, and others—it oxidizes and rusts.

Metals may, for industrial and commercial purposes, be divided into two classes: precious metals and the baser metals. Gold, silver, platinum and iridium are of the former class; copper, brass, iron, nickel, aluminum, zinc, lead, and tin are of the latter class.

Metals left unprotected from the atmosphere would gradually undergo a chemical change. This natural coloration or oxidation sometimes completely changes the appearance of a metallic surface, as will be noticed in old statuary and coins, where time and age alone have given the metal a beautiful patina. No artificial coloring, however, can compare to Nature's process.

But excellent results are possible by mechanical means and chemical compounds. This is only a means of hastening Nature's process. For experimental work in metal

173

coloring the worker should have on hand such compounds and chemicals as potassium sulphide (liver of sulphur), an ounce of platinum chloride (10 per cent solution), tincture of iodine, copper sulphate (blue vitrol), sal ammoniac, oxalic acid, hydrochloric acid, acetic acid, pumice powder, whiting, and bronzing lacquer, formerly known as banana oil.

A piece of silver work may be finished in the following manner: First, anneal; second, boil a minute or two in diluted sulphuric acid, then rinse in water. Third, scrub the work with a brass or steel scratch brush and water; if this is not available fine sand and water will accomplish the same result. This entire process may be repeated three or four times before the metal becomes pure white. It is known as the "brushed finish."

If a little duller finish is desired powdered pumice stone or a kitchen cleanser should be substituted in place of the sand or the scratch brush.

88. Polishing. Rub the surface vigorously with a cloth dipped in tripoli to produce a good ground; then polish with another cloth or chamois dipped in rouge powder or on a cake of crocus. The particles sticking in the corners may be washed off with hot water to which a little ammonia has been added.

Superior work in polishing and scratch-brushing is possible if a lathe or motor is at hand, where revolving brushes and buffer can be used in place of the hand method.

89. Oxidizing Silver. If ordinary care and the following few precautions are taken, very little difficulty should be experienced, and pleasing colors produced.

Clean the work by annealing, then boiling in diluted sulphuric acid, and scratch-brush. It is absolutely essen-

FIG. 152. LAMP
By Mr. Trautmann

tial that the article be made perfectly clean and free from all grease and oil. This is accomplished by adding a little soda to the water when the brushing is done.

The most beautiful finish that can be produced on silver is the platinum finish, a deep French-gray.

> Platinum chloride, 1 gr.
> Distilled water, 500 gr.

Suspend the work in this solution until it becomes tarnished all over, then transfer it to a solution three times the strength of the first one until the desired depth of color is attained. With a little whiting and water on the tip of the finger, rub off in spots to produce the high lights and half-tones. By using a hot solution a different result is obtained from that which comes when a cold solution is used.

A stronger and quicker-acting solution for oxidizing silver is made from:

> 1 fluid oz. tincture of iodine
> ¼ fluid oz. platinum chloride (10 per cent solution)

Apply with a soft brush and let dry. Produce high lights with water and whiting.

A very pleasing gray color on silver may be produced with the following inexpensive solution:

> A small piece of potassium sulphide (liver of sulphur) dissolved in a glass of boiling water.

The work, which must be thoroughly cleaned, may be submerged in the solution until the desired color is produced, rinsed in water, and rubbed off with whiting. If unsuccessful the first time, scrub the work clean and white with pumice powder or some kitchen cleanser and try it once more; no harm is done, and it requires a little practice to get the work to show up in its best possible form. The rubbing off, to produce the proper high lights, half-tones, and shadows, is the most delicate part of the oxidizing process.

If the work contains a stone that is soft, such as turquoise or malachite for instance, care must be taken not to get any of the sulphide solution in contact with the stone as it will absorb the solution to such an extent as to ruin the stone. The stone must be covered with melted beeswax, or the oxidizing solution may be applied to the work with a brush, the latter method being the simplest.

A blue-black color is produced by placing the work in a solution of potassium sulphide diluted with spirit of sal ammoniac until a dark blue-black tone is produced. Wash in water, rub off, and dry.

Green color on silver, according to Lange, may be produced by adding to three parts of boiling water one part of iodine and three parts of hydrochloric acid. Suspend in the solution until the desired color is obtained, then rinse off and rub with whiting and water.

90. Oxidizing Copper. A small piece of potassium sulphide dissolved in a glass of boiling water will make a solution that is commonly used. Any range of color is possible, varying from pale straw, crimson, purple, blue to black. The depth of the color depends upon the temperature and strength of the solution, and the length of time the metal is exposed to its action. Ammonium sulphide and water will produce the same result.

91. Oxidizing Copper or Brass.

A green antique:

> 1 qt. water
> 1 oz. sal ammoniac
> ¾ oz. table salt

This work must be dipped and allowed to dry a number of

times before any effect is apparent.

Green patina on brass or bronze:

   5 pts. water
   1 oz. sal ammoniac
   1 oz. copper nitrate
   ½ oz. calcium chloride
   ¼ oz. oxalic acid
   ¼ oz. copper sulphate

The depth of color may be regulated by adding more copper sulphate and sal ammoniac. This formula is taken from an old German handbook. It was tried out by several students in the author's class and found to work well, giving a great range of shades.

92. **Bright Dip.** Copper and brass may be given a quick dipping in the following bath:

   2 parts nitric acid
   1 part sulphuric acid

and rinsed immediately in clean running water, then dried in sawdust. For a bright dip on silver use carbon bisulfide.

93. **Metal Lacquer.** No metal will retain its color and brightness unless the surface is given a coat of thin transparent lacquer to protect the metallic surface from coming in direct contact with the atmospheric gases, which in consequence will retard oxidation.

There are many metal lacquers on the market in all different colors and shades. A clear metal lacquer is preferable if the original color produced by oxidation or polishing is to be retained.

The work to be lacquered should be warmed slightly to remove the chill. Then apply the substance with a piece of cotton or soft hair brush.

Melted beeswax with turpentine added to make a paste, makes a good surface covering for larger work. When the wax has hardened it should be polished with a clean rag.

What is known to the trade as banana oil may also be used as a substitute for metal lacquer.

TOOLS FOR JEWELRY WORK

1 large alcohol lamp or small gas torch
1 mouth blowpipe
2 pairs of flat-nose pliers, $4\frac{1}{2}$ inches
1 pair of round-nose pliers, $4\frac{1}{2}$ inches
1 pair of tweezers
1 slate for borax
1 jeweler's saw frame, 3 or 5-inch deep
1 dozen jeweler's saw blades, No. 0
1 hand drill
1 charcoal or asbestos soldering block
1 pair of snip
6 assorted gravers with handles
1 small hammer
4 needle files, half-round, flat, round, and bird-tongued
1 draw plate, 40 holes, round
1 engraver's ball, 5 inches diameter
1 horn anvil, 5 inches
1 file, mill bastard, 8 inches
1 file, half-round, 6-inch second cut
1 log, about 12 inches diameter, 24 inches long
1 piece of silver solder, easy-flowing
1 piece of silver solder, hard-flowing
Chaser's pitch (see p. 72)
Chasing tools made from tool steel (see p. 76)
Sulphuric-acid pickle pan (Fig. 7)
1 spool annealed iron binding wire, gage 26

The best and only way to purchase equipment is to send for a catalog from one of the wholesale jewelry supply houses (consult list of Dealers), and select the tools wanted, or see one of the local jewelers in the city. They usually have a catalog on hand from leading wholesale houses and they may even be able or willing to order tools and materials. At times the large houses are somewhat reluctant about sending out an expensive catalog.

An equipment like the one listed here should cost approximately $15.00.

DEALERS

COPPER AND BRASS
 Chas. Besly Co.
  125 North Clinton Street, Chicago, Illinois
 Oscar Krenz
  626 Bryant Street, San Francisco, California
 The American Brass Co.
  Waterbury, Connecticut

STONES
 Klein Bros. Lapidary Co.
  7 West Madison Street, Chicago, Illinois
 Espositer, Vani Co.
  15 Maiden Lane, New York City
 Geo H. Marcher
  934 Santee Street, Los Angeles, California

SILVER AND GOLD
 Thomas J. Dee & Co.
  5 South Wabash Avenue, Chicago, Ill.
 Handy & Herman
  59 Cedar Street, New York City
 Wildberg Brothers
  742 Market Street, San Francisco, California

ART GLASS, PARCHMENT AND GLASS CYLINDERS
 Foskett Co., Inc., Glass Mfg.
  Port Jervis, New York
 Tar Heel Mica Co.
  Plumtree, N. C.

CHEMICALS AND LACQUERS
 Central Scientific Co.
  460 East Ohio Street, Chicago, Illinois
 Waukegan Chemical Co. (Lacquers)
  Waukegan, Illinois

SILVERSMITH'S TOOLS AND SUPPLIES

 Metalcraft Supply Co.

  Providence, Rhode Island

 Wm. Dixon, Inc.

  32 East Kenney Street, Newark, New Jersey

JEWELRY SUPPLIES AND TOOLS

 Swartchild & Co.

  7 East Madison Street, Chicago, Illinois

 Otto Young & Co.

  7 East Madison Street, Chicago, Illinois

 Norton Jewelry Co.

  Kansas City, Missouri

PITCH

 Jared Holt Bros.

  Albany, New York

   or

 Local Shoemaker's Supply House

WROUGHT-IRON ORNAMENTS

 J. G. Braun

  615 South Paulina Street, Chicago, Illinois

INDEX

A

	Page
Alcohol lamp	12
Alloy	17
Annealing	12
Annealing wire	25
Assayers	18

B

	Page
Balls	53
Balls, the making of	128
Ball pein hammer	135
Baser metals	16
Beads	53
Beeswax for transferring designs	11
Benvenuto Cellini	70
Bezels	17, 36, 38
Birth stones	114
Blotter corners	144
Borax	29
Borax slate	30
Bowls	151
Box setting	36
Brass	17
Bright dip	178
Brooch	37
Bronze	17
Bunsen burner	12
Burnisher	12

C

	Page
Cabochon shape	33
Carat	18
Carbon paper	12
Carbonate of copper	58
Carving	50
Catch	40
Chain making	100
Charcoal block	36
Chasing	52, 69
Chasing hammer	53
Chasing pitch	40
Chasing tools	52
Chasing tool, making of	76
Chipping	37
Cleaning by chemicals	13
Cleaning soldering bit	121
Cleaning solution	13
Close setting	36
Coiled wire	25
Composition metal	117
Copper	16
Copper oxide	121
Cracking, risk of	12
Crimping	162
Crucible furnace	116
Crucible steel	76
Cutting links	26

D

	Page
Dapping die	128
Dapping tools	130
Dealers	180, 181
Desk set	144
Design	11

PAGE

Dissolving borax 47
Draw plates 25, 26, 98
Draw pliers 25
Draw tongs 27
Drawer pulls. 128
Drilling 20
Drill, how to make 20
Drill, swiss. 20
Ductile 18

E

Embossing. 69
Exercises in repoussé work. 78

F

File cards 24
Files 23
Filigree 98, 108
Filing. 23
Fine gold 18
Flat-nosed pliers 36
Flat work 124
Flux 29
Flux for soft solder 118
Foot bellow 12
Fusing 29

G

Gages. 19
Gamboge 12
Gas blow torch. 12
German silver 58
Gold 17
Gravers 50

H

Hammered texture 53
Hammered work 124

PAGE

Hand drill. 20
Hand vise 76
Hardening. 77
Hardness 112
Hard soldering. 28
Heat application 38
Heating pitch 47, 74
Horn anvil. 37
Horse stake 165

I

Ingot 116
Inner bezel. 43
Iron binding wire. 32

J

Jamb peg 110
Joints. 40

L

Lantern 130
Lapidary 110
Letter opener 127
Light carving 47
Loam 31

M

Malleable 18
Mallets 154
Matting tools 75
Melting silver 116
Metal coloring 173
Metal lacquer 178
Mica 130
Mouth blow pipe. 12

N

Needle files 24

O   PAGE

Opaque stones 33
Orange shellac 40
Oxidation 29
Oxide 29
Oxidizing brass 177
Oxidizing copper 177
Oxidizing silver 174

P

Paste 31
Pendant 81
Pennyweight 114
Pickle 13
Pickle pan 15
Pierced work 20, 38, 61
Pin vise 98
Pitch 72
Pitch block 70
Pitch bowl 72
Planishing 79, 124, 154
Planishing hammer 124
Pliers, round nose 28
Polishing 174
Porous and soft stones . . . 58
Precautions 12
Precious metals 17
Precious stones 111
Preparation of metal . . . 12
Pulling wire 25
Pumice powder 15
Pure silver 17

R

Raised work 151
Raising hollow vessels . . . 156
Raising tools 75
Refiners 18
Reinforced edge 166

PAGE

Resin 72
Repoussé work 69
Rolling 117
Rouge 31
Ring blank 61
Ring clamp 67
Ring gage 61
Ring joint 61
Ring mandrel 64
Ring making 61
Ring with applied work . . 65
Riveting hammer 126
Rivets 126

S

Sal ammoniac 120
Sandbag 74
Saw blades 20, 23
Saw-frame, jewelers 24
Sawing 20
Scarf pin 54
Scratch awl 12
Scrolls, how to make . . . 107
Seaming 166
Sections of files 24
Semi-precious stones . 111, 112
   Amethyst
   Aquamarine
   Azurite
   Bloodstone
   Chalcedony
   Chrysoprase
   Coral
   Jade
   Labradorite
   Lapis Lazuli
   Malachite
   Malachite azurite

PAGE

Moonstone
Moss agate
Opal matrix
Turmaline
Turquoise matrix
Setting 17
Setting stones 40
Sharpening gravers 51
Silver 17
Silver, how to order. . . . 114
Silver solder, easy flowing 31, 117
Silver solder, hard flowing 31, 117
Slate 29
Snarling iron. 84
Soft solder. 117
Soft soldering 28
Soldering 38
Soldering formulas 117
Soldering iron 119
Spring brass 17
Stake 161
Stamping 70
Sterling silver 17
Stone cutting. 110
Stone polishing. 110
Stone slitting. 110
Stones. 110
Sulphuric acid 13

T

Table of weights 116
Tallow 72

PAGE

Taper. 40
Tapered steel mandrel. . . 37
Temper 20
Tempering. 77
Template 162
Tension 23
Tinning copper bit 120
Tools for jewelry work. . . 179
Tool steel 76
Tracers 70, 75
Transferring a design . . .11, 20
Translucent stones 33
Trays and platters . . 151, 165
Treacherous metals. . . . 13
Tripoli 110
Twisted wire. 65
Twisting wires 108

U

Unit Jewelry. 107

W

Watch fob. 20
Weight of gold. 115
Weight of silver 115
Whiting. 72
Wire brush. 24, 32
Wire and wire drawing . .25, 97

Z

Zinc chloride 119

LIST OF ILLUSTRATIONS

Figure   Page

     Class in metal work 2

1   Steel scratcher and burnisher 12

2   Blow torch and foot bellow 13

3   Gold pendant carved and chased. 14

4   Alcohol soldering lamp 15

5   Gas burner for soldering 15

6   Mouth blow pipe 16

7   Pickle pan 16

8   Wire gage. 18

9   Watch fob 21

10 Designs for watch fobs 22

11 Hand drill 23

12 Drill points 23

13 Jeweler's saw-frame and cutting board 24

14 Clamping the saw blade 25

15 Action of file teeth. 26

16 Cross section of files 26

17 Drawing wire 27

18 Coil of wire tied up for annealing 27

19 Making round links 28

20 Round-nose pliers in use 28

21 Work prepared for soldering. 29

22 Slate for grinding borax. 30

23 Cutting solder. 30

24 Clamping or tying up work 31

25 How to make clamps. 31

26 Wire scratch brush. 32

27 Silver brooch 33

28 Silver pins 34

29 Designs for brooches. 35

30 Making a close or box setting 36

31 Squeezing a setting into place. 36

FIGURE | PAGE

32 Soldering bezel on charcoal block 37
33 Soldering with alcohol lamp 38
34 Stretching a bezel on mandrel 39
35 Horn anvil in use 39
36 Leveling up bezel 40
37 Steps in making a brooch 41
38 Forcing tapered wire into joint and pin 42
39 Block with cement 42
40 Fitting stone into bezel 42
41 A loose inner bezel 42
42 Setting a stone 42
43 Pushing tool 43
44 Setting a stone and tools used 44
45 Work by students 45
46 Silver work by students 46
47 Brooches, light carving and chasing 48
48 Steps in making carved brooch 49
49 Gravers for metal carving 50
50 Engravers ball 50
51 Work being carved 51
52 Chasing tools 52
53 Chasing hammer 52
54 Gold brooch carved and chased 53
55 Artist at work chasing 54
56 Designs for scarf pins 55
57 Steps in making scarf pin 56
58 Holding pin stem while soldering 57
59 Work by students 59
60 Silvercross 60
61 Steps in making a ring 62
62 Ring design with application work 63
63 Scarab ring 64
64 Carved ring 65
65 Swallow pendant 66
66 Silver pendants with moonstones 68
67 Bunsen burner 69
68 Steps in making repoussé work 71
69 Attaching metal plate to pitch 73

Figure		Page
70	Chasing tools	75
71	Hand vise	77
72	Tracing a line with chasing tool	78
73	Repoussé practice work	80
74	Walnut box with applied metal work	81
75	Bell button plate	82
76	Silver brooch repoussé work	83
77	Silver back comb repoussé work	84
78	Pendant designs	85
79	Pendant, iris design, repoussé work	86
80	Silver pendant	87
81	Four brooches, repoussé work	88
82	Scarf pins in repoussé work	89
83	Top panel for jewelry box	90
84	Side panel for jewelry box	91
85	Silver pendant, and two brooches	92
86	Snarling iron in use	93
87	Snarling iron in use	94
88	Hammered silver cup	95
89	Child's drinking cup	96
90	Draw bench	97
91	Making links	98
92	Sawing wire links	99
93	Cutting wire links	99
94	Chain making	100
95	Chains with inserted ornaments	101
96	Lapel watch chain	102
97	Wire unit work	103
98	Wire spirals, how to make	104
99	Twisting a wire	105
100	Filigree brooch from Iceland	106
101	Filigree brooch from Norway	107
102	Coiled wire	108
103	Cutting pliers	108
104	Stones, styles of cutting, sizes and measurements	113
105	Crucible furnace	118
106	The ingot	119
107	Rolling mill	120

FIGURE   PAGE

108　Soldering coppers 121

109　Desk set and book ends. 122

110　Designs for metal book ends. 125

111　Bending metal. 126

112　Riveting 127

113　Letter opener, copper and brass 129

114　Designs for drawer and door pulls 131

115　Straps for drawer pulls. 132

116　Drawer pulls 133

117　Copper drawer pulls 134

118　Waste basket, applied metal work 135

119　Writing desk, applied metal work 136

120　Dapping die and tools 137

121　Wall lantern 138

122　Steps in making lantern 139

123　Lantern with motive for design 140

124　Ceiling lantern 141

125　Riveted lantern 142

126　Lantern designs 143

127　Desk set 145

128　Desk set 146

129　Corners for desk set, the making. 147

130　Desk pad support 148

131　Stationery racks. 149

132　Shallow trays and bowls 152

133　Ball-pein hammer in use 153

134　Mallets and doming log. 154

135　Planishing process. 155

136　Leveling a piece of work 156

137　Punch bowl being raised 157

138　Steps in raising a vessel. 158

139　Raising a vessel by crimping 159

140　Drawing up a piece of work. 160

141　Drawing in the neck of a vessel 161

142　Methods of gaging a line 163

143　Copper tray. 164

144　Platter with pierced design 165

145　Pen tray 166

Figure		Page
146	Steps in making a platter.	167
147	Soldering wire edge	168
148	Seamed work	169
149	Copper candlestick.	170
150	Bud vase.	171
151	Copper candleholder.	172
152	Lamp	175